Winning Strategies for Project Management

Winning Strategies *for* Project Management

The Overlooked Elements

A. MARK MASSEY

ISBN 978-0-692-82480-1

Cover artwork and book interior design by Darlene Massey, DreamSpaceDesign.com

CreateSpace, Charleston SC

.

Table of Contents

Preface

Today the world of business is fast moving, highly complex and interdependent. To be most successful in this modern, hectic era, project management abilities are needed by everyone, not just those holding the title of "Project Manager." In a modern business, small or large, the speed and complexity of internal and external information exchange is amazing. This book is about how to create real world project success and real value in this modern business environment. It is based on firm, successful, "real world" experience.

Project management and good project managers are dedicated to creating value for all concerned. That's what I endeavor to relay to you, how to create real value for all concerned. The exchange for the price of this book is my commitment to bring something of value to you, namely how to create real world project success.

After 30 plus years implementing projects large and small and receiving numerous compliments and commendations, I decided it was my responsibility to share the approaches and techniques I found successful and important. This book shares with you hard won project management lessons using real experiences. Read it and you are unlikely to ever look at project management the same way again. Soon you too will be hearing comments like, "You're the best project manager I have ever seen."

Some may find this book controversial and, in some ways, it goes against the grain of traditional project management teaching. When you read the chapters you will see exactly what I mean.

There are many challenges today to good project management. Modern project managers must keep costs cut to the bone. Sometimes executives try to save money by doing away with project managers altogether. Often they wonder why there are so many problems with the project, why results do not meet their needs, or why the whole thing is just a botched up mess that cost a lot of money and provided little value. The answer is simple, project management skills are required for projects to succeed. Sometimes more skills are required and sometimes less, but project management skills are a key part of creating almost anything of worth.

Companies have been known to use an engineer with great experience and assume they will make a good project manager. Unfortunately, they often do not. Project management is a different discipline than engineering. Certainly some engineers make great project managers, but then they are being project managers not engineers. Project management is different and requires a different skill set.

Any book reflects the education and perspective of the author. I am a person interested in a variety of subjects, some humanities oriented, some business, and some very technical. I think this broad background, including different elements such as religion, business and technology, helped lead to my project management success. My experiences include being an engineer, college professor, shoe salesperson, and a rock and roll drummer.

It is impossible to thank everyone who helped me in the creation of this book, but I can try. I thank my father, Lt. Colonel Jerome Massey and mother, Bernice Massey, for the opportunities given me in our family business when I was young. I deeply appreciate my business and technical professors at the George Washington University, and Stan Grossman who helped me grow professionally at a critical time in my career. I also thank the many outstanding (and not so outstanding) business managers I have worked with and learned from over the years, as well as the technicians and engineers and college students who were, to some degree, my test subjects.

I thank my family and friends who read through the drafts and offered their creative insight and constructive advice: Darlene Massey, my friend and ex-wife, the first editor and layout artist and designer of this book, Fritz Galt, an exciting author in his own right, and an excellent editor. I further thank Brian Wilson for his worthy suggestions and Hannah Schwarz who edited the last version of this text. Finally, I also acknowledge the absolutely amazing Kathy Kleiman who encouraged me to reach the finish line in ways no one else could. I thank all of them for helping me bring the lessons and thoughts of this book to you.

I especially appreciate the individuals who read pre-publication drafts of this book at critical points in their careers. A number of early readers reported back to me that the advice in these pages helped them move from unemployed to employed, and from middle to upper management. I hope their success is yours!

I trust you will find this book valuable in your own life, and when you do, please let others know. Feel free to contact me to share your experiences. My website is markmassey.org. Enjoy the book and may your use of its contents bring you great success in your own careers!

A. Mark Massey
Falls Church, Virginia
July, 2017

Chapter 1

Success in the Real World

> ∿ *On time and on budget when used as the key purpose of a project manager leads to a variety of project failures.*

Excellent project management is critically important to any organization. This book helps you gain the various understandings necessary to become an excellent project manager. Note the word "understandings" in the last sentence—its plural. There are many little parts that make up any body of knowledge. This text makes gaining those understandings a very accomplishable goal.

The information in this book was not developed from a disinterested, theoretical, professorial perspective. It is based upon real world knowledge, won from successful experience (and sometimes unsuccessful experience). It is about how to create success, not how to pass an exam, except the exam of real life.

The intention here is to help you become a success, *not* to demonstrate the breadth of the author's vocabulary! The book is not an expansive tome on the ins and outs of project management software. Yes, to be successful you may need to understand that too (eventually) but first you need to understand *what* you are trying to accomplish as a project manager and *why*.

On Time and On Budget

If you are already familiar with project management then you have probably heard the old mantra that delivering projects "on time and on budget" is the end goal of all project management. Could it be that such a tried and true mantra is lacking. After all, it works perfectly doesn't it? I am certain you have never heard of a software project that was delivered really late or had to be thrown out and redone.

Just think of all of the fabulously successful projects you have been involved with that have run with little problem. Just think of all the software that was implemented on time and on budget. Or how about getting a new computer in an office environment and having it work correctly from the end users' viewpoint the first time they log in. Or Internet based systems that are completely accurate, fully functional (with no broken links), and meet the business needs of their various users. All of these things happening with a minimum of difficulty is an everyday occurrence right? Our society has managing the implementation of high tech down to a "walk in the park," right? If we close our eyes hard enough and put our heads under the covers than the monster in our closet and its cousin under our bed won't bite us.

Repeat after me: "Everything is fine, everything is fine, everything is fine, everything is fine!!!" This is very often the behavior seen in the real world regarding project completion and the creation of value. Unfortunately the old project manager stand by: "On time and On Budget" is horribly inadequate as a guideline a person can truly use to understand *how* to manage projects.

One of the reasons that some companies are shy about investing in technology is so often the money invested has not provided fair value. This is money that could have been profit. There are few business sins as terrible as wasting profit. There is nothing immoral about honest profit. Most people do not really understand what profit is. They may have some idea that it goes to the owners of the company. That is true but functionally there is another very important point.

A Divergence on Profit

Profit is a company's future. Profit strongly affects the resources available to help a company serve existing and new markets. Waste profit and you are destroying tomorrow. This point is lost on almost everyone. It is a critical factor, and is not taught this way in most business colleges. To an accountant profit may be little more than numbers on a paper. To a person who is really managing an organization, profit is the opportunity to do something about any difficult situation the organization is in or to further enhance good situations! If management thinks they can get more profit from investing in something other than technology, then upgrading technology would be stupid or unethical. Therefore some companies have backed off on investing in high tech simply because they have not seen a return on their investment that management considered adequate.

Factually, "On Time and On budget" is the natural result of a properly managed project. But when viewed as the main guiding purpose for projects, "On Time and On budget" has proven itself woefully inadequate.

Do not misunderstand me here. Delivering projects "On Time and On budget" is certainly necessary but it is a natural and native characteristic of successfully managed projects. "On Time and On budget" when used as the key purpose of a project manager leads to a variety of project failures.

Everything is not Fine

Truly, the world desperately needs a fresh and effective approach to managing projects. It is time that we get our collective heads from under the covers and look at what it takes to successfully manage projects and create value for our clients.

Chapter One - Questions to Consider

1. How do you react when you hear there is going to be a major technology introduction at your place of work?

2. How have you seen others react in the same situation?

3. Have you wondered about this reaction?

4. What does the term "valuable technology" mean to you?

5. What does the term "value" mean to you?

6. What is profit?

7. Why is being profitable important?

Chapter 2

The Purpose of Project Management

∾ *The task is largely one of taking advantage of the basic nature of people trying to do a job and managing the environment or the stage these interactions will occur on.*

What is the purpose of a project manager anyway? As noted earlier most texts on the subject frustratingly answer this question in terms of a project accomplished on budget and on time. That is about as useful as guiding a person in matters of the sexes by saying men and woman are different. Yeah – right – no kidding ... now what to do? Heck if I know; this book is about project management. Now let's get back to work. Two key words need to be defined before discussing the purpose of project management. The first word has a special meaning that may already be known by many project managers but since it is an important word, it is defined below for everyone. The word is "deliverable."

Deliverable - that thing which someone is paying for.

- A written study can be a deliverable

- A piece of software can be a deliverable

- A car can be a deliverable

- A set of pans can be a deliverable

- Anything that is being created and exchanged can be a deliverable.

The next word (used later in the text) is "public." The public relations/advertising meaning is the one that applies here, this means a particular group with interests or characteristics in common that make them a single class, or type regarding a particular subject.

- The pro-life public

- The pro-choice public

- The home owning public

- The car buying public

- The computer programming public

A given person is usually a member of many different publics at the same time. For example, I owned an old SAAB convertible that I loved but that I found challenging to do mechanical work on. Thus, I loved the car and was frustrated in maintaining it. I am actually a member of two different publics on the same general topic! This is not an unusual situation. People often have multiple opinions on a given topic.

So what is this about a *purpose of project management*, and what difference does it make anyway? What are we actually accomplishing when we manage a successful project? Is there something in common among all successful projects? What factors were being accomplished in successful projects that were not being accomplished in unsuccessful projects? If one could locate those key factors, and then get those factors accomplished, would that lead to a revised approach that would nearly guarantee project success?

The answer is quite happily, yes! There are key purposes of project management that, if followed, lead to project success. Purposes that lead to the goal of on time and on budget and much, much more!

This statement of purpose came to me one day when I decided to refine all I had learned in thirty plus years of project management down to one sentence. I have never found another statement that was as inclusive yet as simple and *useful* as the one below.

The Purpose of Project Management

The purpose of project management is to manage the creation of the perceptions related to a project as well as to manage the creation of the deliverables of a project

This is discussed with many examples, and in detail a bit further on in the text. For now, just recognize that there are two major purposes:

1. Managing the creation of the perceptions relative to a project.

2. Managing the creation of the actual items to be developed, or accomplishing the things to be accomplished.

The above is a different way of looking at project management than most authors have put forth. What exactly is a successful project manager doing when they are going to meetings and spending hours on the telephone? And why are they doing that? It is vitally important to understand what a project manager is doing. We start our explanation of these questions immediately.

A Project Manager is actually managing creativity. In fact, managing many more creative processes than is at first obvious. Managing these creative processes, and the amazing interplay among these, can culminate in men setting foot on the moon, or magnificent architectural accomplishments, or music and theatre that impact and inspire the world.

Understanding that one is managing continuing creative processes is part of what makes a great project manager great! A Project Manager is managing the widest variety of creative processes. The interactions and relationships that are key natural factors of these creative processes are worth study, and detailed analysis.

As noted earlier this includes managing both the formation of opinions and perceptions about the project while simultaneously managing the creation of the appropriate actual deliverables. The opinions and perceptions regarding a project, and the actual deliverable production form an inseparable duality of value creation.

The Twins

The opinions—perceptions and the actual deliverable production are like a set of co-joined twins or a double bladed axe. Trying to remove one from the other is dangerous and difficult and could easily destroy the viability of both.

So we have the twins but who is the boss? Which is more important? Manage "production" by the numbers or manage the opinions and perceptions?

This is really the critical point discussed in this chapter. One of the hardest things for some people to grasp is that opinion is what creates reality. It is people and their ideas that change the physical universe!

Certainly we may suffer from tight shoes, lack of money etc., etc. but still it is our demand to not have tight shoes that causes us to get them stretched or, better, buy a pair that fits! It is our desires and opinions that motivate us to action!

Most of us are constantly striving to create a better life for ourselves and our children. I have spent time teaching or working in 10 different countries. What is the common thread through all of these societies? People are trying to better themselves and their lot in life that's what!

People work to have things and a better life; who among us does not wish our children a better life than our own. By the way, better does not necessarily mean wealthier. I have known some very unhappy wealthy people. Like beauty, better, is in the eye of the beholder. Thus, if you don't like the amounts of money you are making you are probably at least wishing you could do something about it. If you are reading this book then you *are* doing something about it. You are becoming a more capable project manager. Your opinion and your desires are creating a change in reality. It is you and your motivations that are the source of your life. The results of your actions may take time to show in the physical universe, and your bank account but it is never the less true, that you are creating a change because you want things to be better.

It is your likes and dislikes and your own attitudes toward the factors of life that lead you or anyone else to take action in life and change the world in which you live. Though I may be offending all of the psychologists in the world with these statements, in the real world, it is you who either accepts the hand you are dealt or tries to better it. In the end, it is you who makes your own life. Happiness does not come from being well adjusted; happiness comes from being a successful adjuster!

Things like revolutions occur because enough people got sick and tired of the way things were that they demanded change. An American history college professor said that it only took about one third of the inhabitants of the English colonies in America to create the American revolt against the English Crown. The United States was created by no more than one third of its inhabitants! Those colonists were sick and tired of taxation without representation, high taxes on tea and various absurd trade regulations and other abuses. Eventually they got so frustrated that they risked fortune, life and limb to change it! Their attitude about the whole matter led to the change!

During a Continental Congress Ben Franklin said,"We must all hang together, or assuredly, we shall all hang separately." His comments were simply pointing out that the attitudes of the representatives of the revolting colonists towards one another must maintain a certain minimum degree of agreement or it would mean the end of their effort and their certain deaths. Ben Franklin was no dummy. He knew that he was managing the perceptions and attitudes of the Continental Congress and that it was *vital* because perceptions are what occur before a person is motivated to do something. Perception opens the door to more awareness of a condition and potential action regarding that condition.

No perception equals no awareness. An awareness of a condition occurs before motivation for action. No motivation for action and no change occurs. No desire to change something implies no resources made available to use to create the change and no resources (money) mean no project and thus no job.

An awareness of the need to change something is a critical part of ever getting anything done. Awareness can be managed by managing people's perceptions. If you manage perceptions you are as close to managing awareness as you can get. So how does one accomplish this very high goal of, "managing the creation of the perception of reality"? The first step is to realize that it is there to be managed. This may seem obvious but so many people nearly ignore the issue that it is ridiculous. Nothing is more important than opinions and perceptions as these motivate people to action, yet this critical element is so often ignored in daily management decisions it is shocking.

Changing Opinions

Realize that opinions are going to be created no matter what, it is like breathing. People generally cannot help but have an opinion about all parts of their lives. Work or personal life, people create and have opinions, – just ask. The only question is whether or not you are willing to do *something* about their opinions? If one does not manage this creation of perception and opinion, one is most *unlikely* to have the opinions one wants created. Non-managed creation of opinions is the road of luck. Have you won the lottery lately?

People are constantly responding to and creating opinions and attitudes. Think of the work of a salesperson. Salespersons are totally dedicated to this task. A sales representative may demo a product or service they are trying to sell to you. Why? Quite simple, if you see the thing you are much more likely to agree to its value then by just being told about it. Most of us would probably not even consider buying a car that we had not driven at least once. Is it really comfortable (your opinion)? Does it really have adequate power and handling characteristics for your driving needs (your opinion)? Can you afford the fuel consumption (your opinion)? Does it have enough room (yes, yet again, your opinion)? Does it have adequate styling and panache (obviously, again your opinion)?

By demonstrating the item the sales representative gets you to form opinions and then the sales representative will consult those opinions and either try for the close (get you to sign the papers) or will try to find another vehicle that the rep thinks will more closely suit your needs. In other words, a vehicle of which you will have a better opinion, an opinion strong enough to motivate you to take action. The sale rep is always thinking in terms of how to get from whatever state the transaction is in now to completing the sale. That is their job.

If they do it right, you will feel very serviced and recommend the dealer. If they do it wrong, you may feel very pressured and are unlikely to visit that dealer again. Wrong may mean not understanding your opinions, or being unable to satisfy them, and still pushing for the close anyway (even if your opinions are not favorable). The sales rep's game is find the vehicle that you respond to most favorably, and then find a way to help you buy it. In other words create financial arrangements that suit your needs and wants, in your opinion!

Think of the work of a trial lawyer. One could say a lawyer is being paid to create an opinion of a jury and judge. In the United States if there is reasonable doubt that Joe pulled the trigger (in a juror's opinion) then Joe is not guilty.

In most very high value transactions, people are paying for opinions as well as for things. People buy companies or invest in stocks because they believe (their opinion again) that the company will make them money or provide some other value that they are looking for. You may feel this opinion thing has been beaten to death and to death again. However, it is *that* important! If you learn nothing else from this book but that it is individual opinions that are the motivator for action in life then you have learned something very important and useful, well that's my opinion at least!

So how do project managers create opinions as well as deliverables? How in the world can a project manager do this? There is a lot that goes into answering this question. There are factors relating to human nature, factors relating to understanding legal issues, technical issues, and to money. There are many kinds of factors. Interestingly, from a project manager's perspective, all of these interrelated factors and the things that impact them are best basically viewed as resource management matters. Resources are used to manage perceptions, and to get things *done*. This last point about the fact that resources are managed in a way to create opinion truly deserves illustration. Resources, particularly personnel resources, directly lead to the creation of opinions.

You have probably experienced both good and bad customer service in your life. This is an area where business management often does not realize the depth of impact of their actions on future profitability.

For example, I recently was considering changing cable providers. I was having a certain problem with hooking up my DVD player and powered speakers to the digital video recorder. My son told me it should be done a certain way. I tried that and it did not seem to work. I assumed that I must have made a mistake in doing it, so I decided to try to call the cable company and have them coach me through it. The rep was polite but was basically useless. She kept telling me that this was not supported by the cable company and offered me little help. I eventually said good-bye and hung up and now was definitely thinking about changing companies. Another night I decided, oh well, let's give it one last shot and I called the cable provider back after fiddling around for about fifteen minutes. This time I got a rep on the phone who understood how important her job was. She, too, said that it was an unsupported hook up and that I could not do it that way *but* that if I wanted to, it was very easy to fix by buying a little twelve dollar switch box and hooking it into the circuit. I went and bought the box plugged it in and now I can listen to whatever I want to through the amplified speakers.

If the second rep had helped me in the same way the first rep did I would have been entirely predisposed to change cable companies. This would have cost the cable company one customer (bad - but no big deal) and much worse, since I just happen to have four sections of computer networking students amounting to about 80 students it could have cost the company probably 81 subscribers for both cable and Internet access. Technical students tend to listen to what their instructor's say. Those students have friends too. In fact, the friends of technical students tend to listen to what those students say. It is very easy to imagine what would have happened if a competitive cable company had happened to call shortly after the first less than satisfactory service call. That one misstep could have easily translated into a cost of close to one hundred thousand dollars of revenue for the cable company in one year. Not to mention all of the possible future purchases and marketing opportunities involved here. That is enough to make almost any manager say ouch! PLUS, it would have resulted in the transfer of that revenue to a direct competitor. This is a worst-case scenario for a competitive profitable business! Take profitable customers from company A and give them to company B and you are directly attacking the future of company A.

Profit creates the future. Make no mistake bad customer service can destroy a company's customer base and thus its future. Once again profit creates a company's future.

The point of this story is this: One customer service representative had enough resources invested in her that she was able to provide service to me while the other followed orders and was quite polite but added no real value to the customer support transaction.

After the first service call, I was predisposed to switch to another provider. After the second I am far less likely to switch. These things are my opinions regarding the cable/internet provider situation in my home. They were substantially created by the customer service representatives I dealt with.

They were not created by the technical specifications, nor the channels nor the programming I have access to. In today's market, the vast majority of cable is not exactly an engrossing literary or theatrical experience anyway. Thus, the quality of customer service is a major possible market differentiator between vendors. The actions of the personnel resource in both cases had direct bearing on the creation of my opinion. This opinion creates the circumstances for and provides the motivation for actions. The opinion was created during, and because of my interactions with the resources of the cable company.

Given that people's opinions create reality and you, as a manager, are trying to create the reality you want. It is critically important that you manage the creation of other people's opinions. You must manage the creation of the opinions of your team, your management, your customer's team, and your customer's management. Think big, you may well need to include managing the creation of perceptions and opinions of the family and significant others of all of the above. For example, most married people rarely change jobs without the support or suggestion of their spouse. Most single people have friends or mentors they consult. Ideally, one would create and manage the perceptions of even this extended group.

Oh No! Oh my, that sounds like a precursor to brainwashing or something!

So…yes…your point is…Do you honestly and seriously think you are not being mentally influenced everyday of your life by television advertisers, radio advertisers, your co-workers, your parents, your religious leaders, even the behavior of those around you? One could argue that everyone is trying to brainwash everybody else. Even Baron Von Clausewitz (a Prussian General, advisor and military educator) in his famous treatise on war said the purpose of war is to make one's enemy bow to one's will. Thus, even the unspeakable horrors of war can be seen as simply an effort to change peoples' opinions about the "best" way to behave.

OK, so how does one do this without guns? It is all in managing the interaction of various resources. It is both quite simple and amazingly effective. The task is largely one of taking advantage of the basic nature of people trying to do a job and managing the environment or the stage these interactions will occur on. Set it up so everyone will win and usually everyone will!

The relationship of resources to each other, to outstanding customer satisfaction, to quality control, to professional growth, to profit, to corporate expansion, and to a high level of repeat business is something that is not generally discussed in proper depth, if at all! In fact, demonstrating this interrelationship and how it is created, is a key point of this book, *but* first look again at the purpose of project management:

> ### *The purpose of project management is to manage the creation of the perceptions related to a project as well as managing the creation of the deliverables of a project*

A truly successful project manager never loses sight of the dual nature of this purpose. The fact that this includes managing both the formation of opinions and perceptions about the project, while at the same time managing the creation of the appropriate actual widgets, is absolutely critical.

Management of Opinion

Given the information in other sections about attitudes causing reality, it is obvious that one must manage them. It is somewhat less obvious that one could manage these attitudes in a planned, and controlled fashion. An effective project manager constantly strives to inspire confidence in his or her team, in their customers, in their upper management, and indeed in themselves! One does this by managing one's resources in a way to accomplish both the creation of the perceptions of the project and the creation of the actual widgets!

It is something like a set of expanding boxes. Starting small, with each effort leading in a continuous stream to the next. If you drew this, it might look something like the image on the next figure. The better the perception of the success of an effort, the more likely it is that people will want to work on the effort and similarly the more likely it is that customers and therefore your managers will be willing to invest additional resources in accomplishing the effort. This, of course, means providing real deliverable value to the various publics backing the efforts, as well as controlling the image and perception of the effort.

Good public relations when not backed by solid product delivery turns into a mass of lies. This will destroy you and your project's credibility, and chances for success awfully quickly! A good project manager is always evaluating how a particular action on the part of their team, a client, a supplier, the social and business environment, or even the weather will impact the perceptions and attitudes of the various publics impacted by the project. Everything deserves a little thought. Managing these attitudes create the realities of the project. Manage them first, and managing the actual production of the widgets is much, much easier. Ignore them and manage "production" and the job becomes difficult at best!

For example, say there is a heat wave and one of your personnel is responsible for driving a truck full of records to a client, and the air conditioning in the truck just broke down. You as a manager can react to this situation in many ways. You could say," awe forget it Charlie it is far too hot to drive around in that truck today." You could walk up to Charlie and tell him, "its a tough life, get your butt in the truck, I can always find somebody else to do your job with one phone call." You could have Charlie use your personal vehicle to deliver the records, putting it at risk. You could do nothing. There are a great many ways you could react to this situation. What path do you need to take?

The answer lies in the direction of what will best accomplish the dual purposes of project management. First determine what action is most likely to create the greatest value for your paying publics, and simply compare that to the impact on project personnel. Factors to consider include items like this: is getting those records delivered today important or can it really and truly wait with no impact on the project? This would be rare but it certainly can happen.

What type of a customer are you dealing with? Do they complain when even the littlest non-essential deliverable is not quite on time or are they more flexible? Perhaps you have built enough reservoir of good will with your customer that you can safely invest some in helping a project team member out and sparing him the suffering of a day long trip in 97 degree heat and 95% humidity. That may actually be the better choice for the overall good of the project. There is no pat answer.

The only real answer is to judge all of the factors against the dual natured purpose of project management. One would judge this situation in terms of the various publics and the relative effect on value for each of the publics as well as the relative effect on the perceptions of each of the publics. If your customer is a micromanaging customer who tracks every detail or you are in a situation that these records are, in fact, vital to get delivered right now, well, the records must get through, heat or not!

So let's say that is the situation. The records must get delivered today. What do you do? It all depends. Take a quick look at the personnel resource involved, is he or she likely to suffer heat stroke or have a heart attack from too much electrolyte loss? If not, send him or her, and before you do have somebody fill up a cooler with an electrolyte rich sports drink. Call Charlie on your cell phone and say that life has its problems, but you have something special waiting in the break room and to check it before leaving. Something that acknowledges he or she is doing a bit extra for the good of the team and here is something to make that less painful.

One of the least used and most effective management techniques is the acknowledgement! It generally makes people feel noticed and cared for. More about that later in the chapter on managing personnel but for now let's see how Charlie makes out.

So Charlie delivers the records, has electrolytes, and thinks that you just maybe care a little about his or her life. Charlie drives off less upset and is possibly a safer driver as a result. A single rock in a pond causes many ripples. What you don't know is that while Charlie is dropping off the records he or she mentions to the customer's executive secretary that the AC is broken in the truck and he apologizes for being so sweaty but at least you, the boss took care to supply him or her with cold electrolytes.

For some reason next time you call the customer, the executive secretary is able to suddenly find the executive a bit easier and when you arrive there is coffee waiting for you (maybe the coffee is a bit of a stretch). Maybe you had a bad night and REALLY needed that coffee. It is somehow true that what goes around comes around. It is a strange world.

By your caring attitude and by following the purposes of project management your decisions were guided into doing the best possible solution for the overall good of the team. You have created both the best possible delivery of value and the best possible perception in the eyes of all publics concerned. Perfect!

Certainly, you could have been hard-nosed and just demanded Charlie deliver the records. Most likely, the records would have been delivered too. Charlie probably would not have gotten into an accident because of electrolyte loss – probably.

It is unlikely that Charlie would have treated the Executive Secretary with much courtesy if he was nearly prostrate with heat exhaustion. The secretary would probably think you are just another profit hungry scrooge who did not care about his personnel. In my experience you will surely not be well treated by the executive secretary the next time you need to talk to the executive. Not to mention, I can almost guarantee that the executive will hear something less than advantageous about the situation. You may find yourself handling an upset customer because one of your employees was sweaty and smelly and less than friendly. A far cry from the other scenario!

There are no guarantees in life but this scenario is exactly the kind of thing that happens. Little actions done in alignment with the defined purpose of project management can create big effects. Unfortunately, little actions that are out of alignment with this purpose also create big effects, just not the ones you want!

This is just one example of the relationship of yourself as a project manager to some of your resources and the tasks and business environment you are operating in. Think of the duality of purposes of project management as though it is a shining beacon guiding your way to safe harbor through the stormy night of accomplishing profitable projects! Orient your decisions using the dual nature of project management and your decisions will be generally logical and effective and you will seldom be wrong.

Project Manager - Engineer or Artist?

Often those assigned to the task of project management do not understand the purposes of a project manager. Not infrequently, they were senior engineers in a previous job or have some other tremendous business or technical skill and somehow this elevates them to a level of project manager when they may not belong there. Often they do belong there, often they don't.

Some of the most shocking and fatal project mistakes occur when engineers are managing, when they should be engineering. There goes that controversy again! The point is that a great engineer is neither necessarily a great project manager nor, necessarily, a poor one. When people wearing the Project Management hat fail they usually do so in a very obvious fashion. The project loses money, customer is upset, etc. Fireworks everywhere and sudden mysterious departures. Obvious bad things! When an engineer has reached a level of competence and professionalism that he/she is considered for a management position they usually have an outstanding reputation. To see this go up in smoke is a shocking and amazing thing. Usually, just due to a lack of training in the separate disciplines of Project Management.

In thirty plus years of professional experience I have seen a great many engineers both, degreed/certified and non-degreed/non-certified, these are some of the smartest, most creative people I have ever known. Yet many do not understand or have a feel for the human factors that it takes to build the relationships that business runs on. This is often the genesis of their downfall. Being an engineer is being an engineer. Being a project manager is being a project manager. They are two distinctly different disciplines and *both* are tremendously creative, and when performed to a high enough level, artistic tasks! In fact, you could compare a truly successful project manager to a masterful artist and you would not be far off. A painter paints with color, canvas and brush and the result can be a thing of amazing beauty and inspiration that cause people to stop and stare in awe and wonder. A truly successful project manager paints with resources like money and manpower and the results are a changed world. Indeed, a man walking on another planet is the result of a project manager's work. Every single bridge in the world was built with the help of and guidance from a Project Manager. Never has an airplane flown where the construction project was not project managed. The same thing occurs in the field of the arts only the names change. For example, a producer manages a production.

In truth, a great and successful project manager is one who causes a great many forces to be harnessed. Handles millions of dollars of resources and people, and creates value for the many publics of the project.

These men and woman are real creative masters of the universe in which we live. Without their active work value diminishes to a point that projects are considered failures and are abandoned. These are the people who must put up with the lame paperwork and sometimes frustrating senior executives and all the while keeping their team inspired and perspiring and Go BABY! GO, GO, GO!

Next thing you know there is a rocket on the way to the moon and mankind has accomplished yet another milestone.

A Bit of Personal Belief

It is my personal belief that the successful project manager is the most unsung hero in our varied society. So excuse me if I wax slightly romantic on this topic. Dreams do not get actually created with out *skillful* management of resources that actually get the job done!

It is one thing to have control over resources and use them in a reasonable way to get the job done and create a certain minimum level of satisfaction in your client - to basically manage to get the bill paid without too much overwork nor extensive overtime. This is generally called a successful project. If this mediocrity is success then that explains a lot of what has happened to business in our country.

This is avoiding horrible failure; I would not grace it with the word Success! Remember real success is much more than a bill with the word *paid* stamped on it. This book is about attaining a high level of success!

Real success is customers who tell each other how great your project management skills are; how great your people are, how great your company is; managers who are impressed with your success; and lots of follow on business with your name associated with it! Anything less is just failure avoidance! You will see as you study this approach to project management that failure avoidance is guaranteed if one just works in the direction of accomplishing the purposes of project management!

A project manager is actually a creator of the highest order, an artist of change who uses resources and personnel as a visual artist uses a brush and color. An artist mixes colors to create just the right effect on a piece of canvas. The perfect sunset or a face that shows character are alike created by the skill and desire of the artist. A great project manager blends the skills of personnel and other resources to create the right effect, to create an outstanding perception of value and real delivered goods and services.

Probably the one way to examine project management in depth (after understanding its purpose) is to study a project's life cycle. A project's life cycle is simply the sequence of how it starts, progresses, changes, and eventually comes to an end. It needs to be understood as a progression of real world events, not just as a theoretical series of stages that occur in a pleasantly predictable sequence. We start addressing these, at times, mysterious and difficult to predict events in the next chapter.

Chapter Two - Questions to Consider

1. *How do people try to influence your opinion every day?*

2. *Is it morally wrong to influence others minds?*

3. *What does opinion have to do with war?*

4. *What are some of the characteristics which people share that you trust?*

5. *How do you feel when you have accomplished an important goal or project? Does this make a difference in your willingness to take on the next task?*

6. *What does value have to do with opinion?*

7. *What is the difference between real value and perceived value?*

Chapter 3

The Project Life Cycle

⤳ Most successful larger projects are almost organic in nature with different parts growing and shrinking along the way to actually create the value the customer really needs and wants.

A Brief Introduction to the Project Life Cycle. Projects have a life cycle. This is the series of steps or phases. According to the Guide to the Project Management Body of Knowledge from the Project Management Institute, the basic phases of the project life cycle are:

- The inception or idea

- Bringing the project to fruition

- Starting the project and executing control

- Closing the project.

The approach to project management recommended in this text looks at these project phases as evolutionary phenomena that naturally occurs in a well run project. In other words, these four phases naturally evolve one to another with a great deal of overlap and feedback. If a project manager tries to manage with these four steps in a strictly linear approach, he or she will bungle the project.

It would probably be most accurate to consider these four phases as conditions of existence in a project rather than as steps one takes. A larger project is constantly evolving. Work is being done, specifications change, funding is added (or removed). It is a constant evolution. It is appropriate and useful to define these four steps as conditions that some part of a project is in. It is positively detrimental to consider these four conditions as phases that occur in lock step one after another. In the real world it is your job to push a project forward and help it mature through these natural evolutionary phases by creating value throughout each step.

In some ways, it is more like the task of a parent guiding the growth and moral fiber of a child. You see the child make strides one day and the next there is a half step backward. As a parent, you fix whatever it is that is halting the growth (if you can) and the child gets back on the road to maturity and self-sufficiency. These four conditions are unlikely to occur throughout the entire project in a perfect linear fashion. In fact, if they do it is a most unusual project or you are not doing your job.

A big part of managing a project is managing the change that occurs (or should occur) in a project. Change is the critical phenomena. It is possible that even in the final condition of a project (closing the project) that the consumer of a project will add other requirements such as new documentation. Thus, the idea that these four conditions are set in stone, unbendable, and occurring one right after the other is just not a reflection of real business life.

These four steps are a convenient general categorization. They are effective and useful names for the general activities that are going on most at a particular time in a project, but as noted above even in the last of these four conditions the project can change.

This text will put most of the reader's attention on creating a successful project environment and managing the change of that environment. Ideally, the reader will see these different conditions as part of the natural evolution of a project. Successful larger projects are almost organic in nature with different parts growing and shrinking along the way to actually create the value the customer really needs and wants.

Since these four conditions of project maturity provide a useful framework for discussion, we will start with a discussion of the first of these conditions. It is a critical time in the life of a project.

The Inception or Idea

The beginning is the inception or the idea. What is interesting is how this phase sets the stage for the rest of the project. In some ways, it is like the opening scenes of a play. Usually fairly quickly, the key actors are introduced and the initial subject of discussion is revealed.

There can be a number of key players. Each of these folks is fundamentally a public (see Chapter 2). Among them are:

- The Dreamer – the original source of the idea

- The Inside Salesperson – the idea's champion

- Various Sales Representatives and possibly their technical advisors

- Customer Project Manager (ideally will be involved at this point but is often not)

- You - the Project Manager (ideally will be involved at this point but you are often not)

Since the above mentioned key players are the source of what occurs, their activities are critical. The following discussion will consider some of the factors relating to each of these roles. We will start with the role of the Project Manager and touch on all of them.

Creating Value at Project Inception

A project manager's perspective on a project should always be on how to successfully create value. Of course, this comes about through the management of the factors leading to the creation of perceptions and as well as the creation of real life widgets.

The project manager needs to be in a position where he/she can control the project to create maximum value for the projects various publics. With no control, it is impossible to manage. Therefore control is a must.

It has been said that the best possible time to gain control of something is when that thing is small and easy to control - when there is not too much going on. This applies very, very truly to projects. The best time to get control of projects is before they exist! What is this wacko talking about now the reader wonders? Controlling something before it exists – hmph!

Let me explain with some graphic (yet pleasant) childhood memories. I remember being a small boy in Fairfax County Virginia before it became a major high tech center. There were still cows from neighboring farms in the yard in the morning and things like that. One of the things the neighborhood kids used to absolutely love to do was to build dams across creeks. We were definitely trying to control the forces of nature. We were serious competition for some of the beavers in the neighborhood. I am sure the EPA would have demanded environmental impact statements for some of our larger efforts!

There was a whole lot of construction around at the time, Fairfax was going through massive growth, and enterprising kids from about 6 to 16 years of age could always "find" a few boards or cinder blocks or whatever they needed to challenge nature. Most of the time we even had permission to "borrow" our supplies. After all, construction workers usually appreciate kids building things since that is what they do themselves.

We would take on creeks and Mother Nature left and right. There was one particular adventure where we addressed a creek and gully between what we thought were Civil War train tracks. This was a beautiful place for a dam. The banks must have gone up at least twelve feet on each side. We tried several times to dam that creek and it was very hard. Whenever we tried to dam the thing, the waters would just have too much pressure before we were ready and boom - there went the dam and probably a good twenty kid hours of effort too. We learned many lessons that I have found also apply in life, particularly useful in the management of high tech life!

We realized it is much easier to divert the course of a small stream than a broad creek; it is easier to divert a broad creek than a river, a small river than a larger one, etc., etc. We won too. After a number of catastrophic and disappointing failures we realized we needed to control the force of the water very early in the project while we were laying the base for the next level of construction. We diverted water to keep the pressure on our dam low while it was being constructed. In essence, we got control of the water early by directing it where we wanted it rather than by stopping the flow altogether. Eventually we had built ourselves a dam that was every bit of four feet high, maybe taller (maybe smaller – it was a long time ago seen through the positive and brilliant eyes of a child)!

You as a project manager need to be involved in the project as early as possible. The easiest time to control it is when the forces are small, and that is early in a project. This is usually in the marketing and sales phase.

Managing Your Salesperson

Since we are discussing inception, let's look at the sales process for a moment and its main ingredient, the various salespeople. There are some things that you, as a project manager, must understand about sales! Salesmen/Saleswomen are critically important parts of any organization. One must remember that their job is to SELL above all else! There is an old saying that my grandfather taught me, "nothing happens until something is sold," it just happens to be true! So always, always, always take care of your salesperson!

Senior management also needs sales and income above all else! They are responsible for profitability; no matter how great your project management skills and your teams' technical skills, no sales equals no projects, thus no opportunity to create a profit. No profit means no money available for future investment. This means no money available for marketing, nor for training on the latest products and tools, nor income to pay salaries. If this goes on for too long it means you are lost!

Sales runs the world and so it should be but still… sometimes in the process of closing the sale and getting the order, sales representatives have been known, shall we say, to not bother to expressively mention the limitations of a product or service. This can create surprising customer expectations. (*I am* trying to be gentle!)

As a project manager your job is to deliver the goods above all else. There are times when the two objectives of sales and project management will not see the world in quite the same way (severe understatement). This is a senior management problem; senior management should address it, but commonly it is not well addressed. It *is hard* to face up to and deal with! It has to be dealt with and the sooner the better. In many organizations the one who first confronts this problem is, in fact, the Project Manager. This means *you*!

Thus, early management is important because early management is much easier to accomplish than later management. The critical thing to manage early is customers' expectations. The key to accomplishing this, is the early management of that which is creating the customer's expectations, the sales rep!

Manage your salesperson and their presentations and your customer's expectations will be something within the realm of reason. This is not necessarily easy but it can be important and can help lead to sales and project success. You can coach a salesperson into not promising unattainable realities but rather into stating the real features and benefits that you and your company offer. This is usually what the sales rep should be selling anyway.

High ticket items are usually purchased based as much upon confidence as upon specifications! Thus, if you can, manage the salesperson before the they have a chance to "accidentally" make the customer believe that the network you are installing comes complete with the sun, moon, and stars, and will absolutely raise the customers productivity by xyz percent all by itself. This would, of course, be ridiculous and is nothing but a bunch of, uh …well, sales talk. Keeping the salesperson's promises under control will help tremendously as the project progresses through various phases of implementation.

A real story may illustrate several of these points. The names and location are changed for privacy. Once, I was working as a sales engineer for one of the largest computer companies in the world. A sales engineer can have various duties; key among them is usually helping to ensure the overall value or deliverability of a project from the beginning.

We will name my sales rep Elliot and the customer information technology executive Don. Don was the IT Director for a major east coast city. This city had bought millions of dollars of goods and services from the company Elliot and I worked for. I was originally called in to the account to fix a customer relationship problem. This problem was cause by an unrealistic customer expectation regarding the performance of a particular computer program which was fairly new to the market. Truly adequate performance required more computer memory than the customer had bought. Thus, the customer was very upset with the performance of the system.

I eventually discovered that we had already recommended a more appropriate amount of memory to the previous IT Director who was now apparently unavailable for comment. In fact – he was behind bars for embezzlement! Through some technical and presentation skills, I demonstrated to Don that lack of computer memory was the real problem. This was done in a way he could understand and that did not make him, or anyone else, look like an idiot (except the now departed former IT Director who was not held in high repute by anyone). This created trust between the IT Director and me. In fact, our company went from a threatened law suit to being asked to submit more bids for additional goods and services in one week. This was darned good work, even if I say so myself! Now what comes next is really unusual!

Elliot and I were in Don's office and Don asked about some capabilities that were theoretically possible but were very infrequently implemented in certain network hardware. At this point Elliot (the sales rep) starts his mouth running,"... oh yes *certainly* we can implement that – no problem at all, etc!" I said something like this to Elliot (the sales guy) in front of Don (the IT Director), "Elliot we need to verify exactly how that will operate in this environment before we make too many promises."

Didn't slow Elliot down one bit! He was a freight train going downhill! I then said to Elliot, "I really need to verify with the manufacturer regarding this environment before we make any guarantees." Elliot was busy selling used cars or something. I could see Don's eyes start to change back to the old "I'm going to kill you" look. I decided – oh what the heck, my job is on the line if I say something or not. May as well do the right thing. Right there in front of the customer, I said *"Elliot – Shut UP!!"* Don breaks out laughing, Elliot is standing there shocked and Don reaches into his drawer and pulls out a bunch of candy and hands it to me and to Elliot!

He says to Elliot, *"Mark has earned this. He has earned my trust. Now I absolutely know I can trust him! I never want to see you in my office again without him. I expect a proposal on my desk next week for the new hardware and services."* As I recall it, we sold him another half a million dollars worth of gear and services in the following months.

It was quite a risk I took – yes, a dangerous one but I knew that this customer was *not* going to put up with more unbridled verbal galloping of a sales rep without harming the trust I had built up. To Elliot's eternal credit, when we were alone he turned to me and said, *"You can kick me in front of the customer whenever you need to. Just keep the requests for proposals and sales coming in!"* Elliot was good enough to know a good thing when he saw it! Effective sales reps are so cool they amaze me! To them it is all about getting the sale!

For me, it was all about managing the customer and his expectations, managing my sales rep and the overall presentation and preventing another problem.

Thus, this particular time, I had early access to the salesperson and the sales cycle and I knew it needed to be managed right now and badly – so I did it. My actions appeared to be a risky choice – I expected it to come out just fine or I would not have done it. It was much more risky to do nothing !

In this situation early access meant firm and effective control of the sales cycle (for the new hardware/software) and *this* put the whole project on a truthful and respected basis from its beginning. I created more confidence in my company as a whole and in my customer's mind. He knew he had the sales rep whenever he needed him already, now he also knew beyond a doubt, that he had a technical sales engineer who would shoot straight with him to the best level of his ability even if it meant taking some personal risks! I have never known an IT Director who would not give his left arm for that type of relationship with his vendors.

So, that is a useful example of managing a project at its inception.

The Dreamer, the Inside Salesperson and Marketing

This example showed true project inception - someone has an idea and contacts some vendors regarding the idea. It all starts with an idea.

The idea may be a way to save money, to increase competitiveness, to meet a legal requirement, to enhance security, or just as a way to spend some money and try to look good (as unbelievable as it sounds that happens all the time!). So we have a dream and where there is a dream, there is a dreamer. Ah yes, there is the source of the project. The real source is the person with the dream, not some bureaucracy or department or agency or something.

It is always a living person – know this is true and it will help you as time goes forward.

Next we have an inside salesperson. Somebody has to sell the idea to other people to get approval and funding. This may or may not be the original dreamer. Even corporate presidents like agreement among other senior executives (and all staff for that matter) that a particular project is worthwhile. Though we seldom think about it, very capable people are frequently after the president's job. The inside salesperson can be anyone from the Chairman of the Board on down. Part of the intelligence a project manager needs to gather is *who* is the dreamer, *who* is the inside salesperson and *why* was the project approved. If the project is major, these little pieces of information can be of great use later. So find it out, document it, and set it aside for later.

There are situations where major projects have been approved substantially as a smokescreen for a smaller project that desperately needed to be done but would stick out like a sore thumb to competitors and regulators if that was the only project funded. When things seem illogical they usually are and you need to know why. Again, you set this information aside for later. You may not even wish to document it as it can be too sensitive.

For example, a company may have a major security problem with its network. They want this kept confidential for a variety of reasons. Therefore, instead of putting out bids to the world to fix their security problem (thereby advertising it to everyone!), the company may put out a bid for some new network gear they would like anyway and by the way, security is to be enhanced too. Actually, the network gear could have waited but the security hole could not! Thus, the company gets the security problem fixed without calling attention to its existing inadequacies.

There is this old saying from the world of military security: "Loose lips sink ships." This means that if you talk casually about secret information such as what route your vessel is going to take, a spy may hear it. This could lead to an enemy submarine waiting along your path to destroy your ship. Sometimes this is also true in business. "Loose lips" can sink careers too!

Rumors have been known to affect the price of a company's stock. This can mean millions of dollars to individuals. Make somebody loose a couple of million dollars because you talked too much at the bar? That could be the subject for a book, "How to ruin your career in one easy lesson." No thanks, keep it quiet and private. Not to mention, you, personally, may be sued for breach of fiduciary trust as well as your firm for breach of contract regarding information obtained in confidence. This is real and serious stuff and can be more important than anything else about a project.

Okay, beyond our dreamer and the inside salesperson (possibly the same individual person) who else is involved? Next, usually there are one or more sales reps for providers of the goods and services that are being purchased. These may be your friends and competitors. Business, politics, and war make strange bedfellows! You may be in a situation where your company loses the bid as the prime contractor but the buying customer likes your proposal so much that they instruct the winning contractor to use more of your personnel and plan than you thought possible. Sometimes the other contractor "wins" but most of your company and most of your personnel keep their jobs!

For this to occur easily you must maintain friendly relationships with your enemies. Business is funny - particularly in contracting to the government and the large contracting industry. It is not at all unusual for the same contracting technical personnel to work for a particular government agency for an entire career or certainly for a large percentage of a professional career. After some period of time the contractor personnel may know more about the way the job is done than the people who "oversee" them.

It can get pretty funny sometimes. Talk about politically sensitive - whew! Walk softly on those eggshells (they are scattered across rice paper and rice bowls).

So, you must maintain contact with your enemies – always at a pleasant arm's distance of course. I think it was Machiavelli who said that the safest place for one's enemies was close by. That way you always know what they are doing. That is an idea at least worth noting in these situations.

This brings us back to the "enemy" sales reps. Talk with your sales rep about them. You need his/her guidance on this matter. If your sales rep is good, they will probably know or at least be trying to get to know the competition as soon as possible. You should definitely know the personnel of competitors; try to have social contact with them at user group meetings and the like. But don't talk much business. You can talk shop but not business. There is a difference. Shop talk is technical, "What's up with product XYZ?," that kind of thing. Business talk is more like, "Did you hear that one of the VPs is planning on leaving." Or perhaps, "I understand that the Department of Homeland Security is getting ready to issue a bid for new whats-sa-thingies."

Get to know their personnel, their technical strengths and their weaknesses. You can listen for others talking business – that's their problem not yours. Of course, you may be lucky and stumble across a junior engineer who is trying to look important and who overheard some meeting information. Who knows? You just may find some very interesting information about their marketing strategy or internal company news that your competitor would prefer you did not have. Perhaps key personnel ripe for the plucking…We will talk more about gaining business intelligence when we talk about personnel in a later chapter.

Bringing the Project to Life – Feasibility Studies and Proposals

Now let's get back into the meat of the first of the Project Management Institute's four project phases - Project Inception. Normally, when personnel in a company have agreed to go forward with an idea they start asking for requests for information or perhaps requests for proposals from potential vendors. This is, in essence, the same process you go through when you consider servicing your vehicle.

For example, say your car is killing batteries and the folks at Sears have told you that their Die Hard car batteries are dying hard because your alternator is not recharging the battery properly (an alternator charges the battery in most automobiles). This problem requires solution. The desire to have this problem solved is the motivation behind the idea to get the alternator fixed. This leaves you with several choices and you have to figure out what to do. Your options might be:

1. Bring the car to the dealer and get a factory certified mechanic to do it.

2. Get a non-factory certified but still certified mechanic to do it.

3. Take it your friend Bubba and see if he can help you.

4. Buy an alternator and install it yourself.

You have to make up your mind. To "make up your mind," may likely require the gathering of certain types of information to study the feasibility of the project. Now, say you are capable with a wrench and can change oil and have a basic understanding of vehicular maintenance. Then you have a set of judgment calls you need to make. For example:

1. How complex is this job?

2. Is this job within my skill set?

3. Do I buy a new alternator, a rebuilt one, or perhaps a used one?

4. What is the cost of each type?

5. Where can I buy one?

It is worthy of note that in developing the answer to each of these questions you may have to do research. If you have just changed a similar alternator, the research could be as easy as a call to your local auto parts store for cost and availability information. You already have answered questions one and two above through your experience. However, prices may vary and availability certainly does. Try looking for a part for a twenty-year-old SAAB some time and you will see what I mean. Then, having gathered the information to answer 1 through 5 above you can formulate the beginnings of a plan to accomplish changing the alternator yourself.

The above process is the same basic thing any business or organization does when it is evaluating the implementation of an idea. What are the idea's costs, benefits, and risks? Senior level managers ask themselves these questions every day. Indeed, we all ask ourselves every day about one thing or another in our lives. Whether it is going out at night or making a certain investment, we are all trying to predict what will be best for our future. Most of us do that by gathering data and then making our best guess.

Individuals in business management do the same thing. Organizations issue Requests for Information (RFI) to study the feasibility of a project and Requests for Proposals (RFP) to study the predicted costs of a project in depth, the timing, and the resources and approaches that experts might take to accomplish the project. Then, in theory without bias, a winning combination of cost, benefit, and risk is proposed by a vendor and the next thing you know, we are spending money on lawyers to review a contract. Eventually, if all goes well, we have a new contract and a new project getting started. Congratulations!

The aforementioned proposal took a lot of project planning. A project manager simply figured out the sequence(s) that things need to be done in, to accomplish a goal, figured out the resources required to get these things done, the timing, etc. Interestingly, resources, their types, their utilization, and their control is featured throughout this text because it is resources that create the changes a project manager is trying to make!

Except one little problem….the above process (idea, RFI, RFP and contract award) took from two months to two years (no joke!) or possibly even longer.

Early Analysis of the Signed Contract - The Vital First Step in Managing a Contract

The last section pointed out that it can take considerable time to get a project plan created, approved, funded, and finally have a contract put in place. Taking years is not unusual in a large organization for a large contract. The only constant is change and usually the more time there is, the more change there is. Thus, it is quite common that what someone finally contracted for (bought) is far from what they now need!

Oh joy! So now we have the following situation:

1. A customer with a substantial amount of authorized funding.

2. A contract that may be inappropriate for the real needs of the customer because of the time that was added by budget processes, lawyers, holidays, vacations, births, deaths, and the summer solstice – it is amazing how many things can slow getting a signed contract.

3. An original project plan that has little to do with reality.

4. A customer with a real need that has evolved from the original need.

5. Management on both sides of the contract that are grossly unaware of how messed up the whole scenario is.

The above situation arises with horrible frequency. It is most likely to occur when project managers have been in an organizational model that does not allow them to have early input into the sales process or when the entire process takes a long time. Therefore, be aware that very early on, you must meet with your customers and find out what they actually bought versus what they *think* they bought versus what they wish they could have bought. In the real world what they tell you will almost always be at variance, in greater or lesser degree, to what your company thinks it sold! This may sound amazing but it is true.

This is really an opportunity for you to shine like the sun! You can straighten out this mess, gain your customer's trust, gain your managers' trust and be a local hero (for a little while anyway).

Contracts are made to be modified. Contract modifications are actually a customer's and project manager's best friend!

Please recall the purpose of project management:

The purpose of project management is to manage the creation of the perceptions related to a project as well as to manage the creation of the deliverables of a project.

Please once again note: The purpose does not say deliver the contracted goods on time and on budget. As noted earlier the situation almost always changes from the time an idea is created to the time the actual project is started. If you robotically follow the contract, most of the time you will not, in fact, accomplish the purpose of project management. There is a chance you might be paid, as there is a legal document in place, but you can forget about references and follow on business - where the real money is made.

How can a project manager create value at this moment in the project's life-cycle? It's darned simple to say, challenging to do and critically important to do well.

Creating Real Business Value through Contract Modifications

Find out what real value would mean for this client in anything related to the original contract through the process of friendly communication and investigation, and make the contract reflect the real value through contract modification. This will lead to more customer and contractor success than almost any other step of the process. This is true because you are setting the agreements for what is to come and these agreements are the ones that the customer has said will best help their survival *now*.

Yes, you also have to see to it that the contract docs are modified to reflect the real world. To do otherwise is not just sloppy management - it is a treasonous act against your own company. Remember, all that your group can easily demand to be paid for is what the customer has agreed to in a legal and binding document. Handshakes and smiles are part of business and quite pleasant indeed but generally are not worth much when compared against a written contract in a court of law.

So caution here and now

If the customer refuses to modify the contract when it needs to be modified, then something is very wrong. The customer may be trying to get something for nothing. There is a word for that, *stealing*. It is not good business. It is stupid and dangerous and I urge you to say good-bye to that customer ASAP! Some customers will try to get something in addition to what they agreed to pay for. A little bit of that is expected and allowances for it should be built into every bid but it is still dangerous territory!

Remember, if you give a customer what they ask for and it is not specifically called out in some sort of contract there is no reason that the customer should pay you beyond their being a nice fella. If they were nice fellas why wouldn't they agree to a contract modification in the first place?

The customer is trying to shift the rules to a no win situation for you personally and for your company. We are not talking about fair exchange here, we are talking about not playing by the rules and ruining the game. No fair! The safest thing to do is to fully document the situation, start looking for another job, and present the case to your management. You will probably be fired (it will be called a reduction in force) unless you have extremely bright management. If you are well respected (meaning they are smart enough to recognize the situation for what it is) they will at least try to find something else for you to do because you have just saved the company volumes of pain and problems. Some customers really are crazy and you don't need them!

None of this means that you don't have to sell the idea of contract modifications to your customers. Often, they have never done it before and afraid of it. It is very important that the specific process of contract modification is clearly documented in the original contract.

We will discuss matters relating to contracts further in the section on contracts. For now, I hope you get the idea that the situation is normally messed up at the beginning and this is often your first opportunity to shine. Become a hero by taking control of the situation and impress both your customers and your management with your care and effectiveness as a project manager. Remember you are being paid to do this so just do it! You are creating a huge amount of value and showing a very high level of care for your customer by refusing to let them spend their money on the wrong thing!

So, the major lesson here is that before you invest yourself in accomplishing the project be sure that you have the customers' agreement that what you are trying to deliver is what they really want. This is a major step toward accomplishing managing of the perceptions of a customer. By doing this you have shown that you cared enough to fight this battle and that you really want them to get their money's worth. That, by itself, should have made your customer think of you more as an ally than as a barbarian there to steal their money, take their food, and generally not deliver the goods. Thus, you are influencing perceptions. In addition, you have the added benefit of now having gained a much greater depth of understanding of what the customer needs and wants and why. You will probably also gain a favorable introduction to the customer's management team.

Normally, your own managers will also be impressed that you have a clearer understanding of what the customer wants, too. Finally, this will give you some visibility to the corporate lawyers and other executive managements in your own firm because modifying contracts usually requires review of at least one lawyer.

Again, this creates an opportunity to quietly shine with your presentation and customer care skills. At this point, you are exchanging both internally and externally to your organization by adding the value of a real, desired, and accomplishable project as opposed to some, unaccomplishable nightmare that no sales rep should have sold, nor some project that the customer barely cares about.

Very well done!

We have discussed inception fairly well from an organizational factors viewpoint. What's next? Step two of the model - Planning to bring this idea into fruition.

Chapter Three -Questions to Consider

1. *What is a sales person's role?*

2. *Why do sales persons have clout?*

3. *How should a project manager handle a sales person?*

4. *In a corporate situation, who is likely to get fired first, a successful project manager or a successful sales person?*

5. *What should you immediately investigate once you have a signed contract?*

Chapter 4

An Overview of Project Planning

> ∿ *The single most amazing and interesting thing about planning is to realize all of the different resources that you have to plan to control ... The key is in how much attention to detail is placed on certain factors throughout the project life-cycle. Timing is everything.*

Planning is truthfully an alchemist's blend of communication, estimation of resource utilization, sequencing of actions, expecting the unexpected, and dealing with it – while always keeping the dual-natured purpose of the project manager as the active guiding principle. Nothing is more important than that. The other factors are discussed to help accomplish project management.

What is one actually doing when planning a project? One is simply laying out the most efficient interaction of available resources to accomplish a goal. Successfully planning a project involves using more of one skill than any other. That skill is communication. Why would the ability to communicate be so important? The simple reason is that there will be a tremendous amount of communicating! You will be negotiating the availability of resources, initial explanation of the task, getting technical estimates, ensuring any necessary customer resources will be available, adjusting schedules and generally seeing to it that everyone is on the same page. Communicating, communicating and communicating some more.

Planning is where computer based project management can really be helpful. The popular tools of a project manager are very useful in figuring out man hours of specific resources, the associated costs, schedules and sequences of events. When used properly, the graphs these tools produce can be tremendous aids in planning and communication. The old saying that a picture is worth a thousand words is very true in the world of project management! If there are substantial mis-communications at this stage of the project, it will create a tremendous amount of work and difficulty later as the project matures.

Thus, an in-depth understanding of the types of resources involved in a project is critical to your success. Below is a brief introduction of this topic. The next several chapters discuss various types of resources in some detail.

Resources – The List

The single most amazing and interesting thing about planning is to realize all of the different resources that you have to plan to control. So what exactly are the resources we are managing? The following list looks long but do not let it scare you!

As we will see later, these resources are not actually hard to manage, if it is done right. But on the other hand you must *realize* that these resources are what you are managing, otherwise one factor or another will pop up most unexpectedly and damage your project, your success, and your reputation!

We will address each one of these resources in some detail in subsequent chapters.

1. Communication

2. Money

3. Time

4. Widgets (software, computers, furniture, radios, robots, whatever items might be involved in getting the project done)

5. Personnel

6. Your boss

7. Your boss's boss

8. Your team members

9. Your managers (if any), the ones who report to you

10. The above managers' personnel

11. Your customer's project manager

12. Your customer's project manager's boss

13. Your customer's security management personnel

14. Any customer members of the team

15. Your customer's commitments to you

16. Political Capital – Political capital can be defined as all of the various factors that add up to making others want to actually do something to help the project succeed.

17. Legal Factors (agreements to accomplish or have accomplished for us).

    - Examples: A Statement of Work (the agreement stating what is to be done and for how much money)

    - A letter of agreement or intention

    - Modifications and addendums to a contract

18. A project plan

19. Risk

20. Risk management strategies

21. Schedules

That is about 20 different categories of activities/things to manage. Now for the good news: If you set it up right, you will not have to do very much to manage any single one of these categories at a particular time. The key is in how much attention to detail is placed on certain factors throughout the project life cycle. Timing is everything. Manage the right factor at the right time and all will be well. Put your attention on the wrong factor many times and your project will definitely suffer. These resources and how they relate to one another are discussed in a series of small sections and chapters as we proceed.

Chapter Four – Questions to Consider

1. *Why would it be useful to the project manager to have a list of the categories of resources that must be managed?*

2. *Does a project manager have to manage over twenty different resources at the same instant?*

3. *What are the key reasons to use project management software?*

4. *What one ability is most crucial to a project manager's success? Why?*

Chapter 5

Communication

~ *To communicate effectively, one must start with an initial willingness to be listened to on the part of the audience.*

Communication is, without a doubt, the most important thing that exists in the field of human relationships. Indeed, if you extend the concept it even can be shown to be at the heart of life itself. Pretty amazing. One does not have to be the greatest expert on communication the world has ever seen. One has to get along OK and that is truly all that you generally need to do. But you must *always* accomplish at least that! And *that* can be a challenge!

If you just care enough that what you wanted communicated was, indeed, communicated and ensure that what Joe thought you said, was what you intended, then most things will work out fine.

The overall point is that you as a manager must truly understand exactly what you are telling people and what people are telling you. Once in a while, this can be much harder than it looks but is *always* of great importance to get right. Before the misunderstanding and upset there is very frequently a miscommunication.

Communication and Image

Another point that falls into this category with a huge *thump* is the concept of *image*. Here we go back into the art of Public Relations again. Some people say, "Image is everything." Well, it is not, but it *is* very important because of the mental reaction factor again.

Image is a single word that is a summary for a number of factors all of which amount to what status does someone think you deserve. In one second (or so) people look at you and make considerations about you. This may be quite unjust and the result may be unfortunate. But people almost always do this.

The point is that image sets certain expectations regarding the life and times of the observed. In essence, what is happening here is that one's image is used by another person to make a mental calculation. The observer will make thoughts about the observed cash condition, happiness, education, family life, etc. This calculation correlates the experiences that a person has had with the way people now appear.

In sales this phenomena is sometimes called "qualifying by the seat of the pants." Here is an example: Salesperson X watches a potential customer come in the door. Perhaps this potential customer is dressed poorly and appears to be carrying a bottle in a bag. The good sales rep *will not* just decide "That guy is an alcoholic, and has no money, why should I waste my time, and energy and my opportunity to make some money." The good rep will take the time to politely find out if this person can be helped.

It is seldom that people will go into "expensive" stores with no hope of being able to purchase. I have seen paper bags that looked like they belonged to drunks that instead contained a root beer bottle and thousands of dollars in cash. The owner did not happen to like banks (his opinion) and discovered that when he was out shopping and looked less than successful he was not a target for thugs and was less bothered by store personnel who did not really care. He was actually quite wealthy and he felt this camouflage gave him security.

I talked to the fellow and sold him a substantial amount of goods - not qualifying from the seat of my pants. I did not let my preconceived notions (my opinions and expected agreements) get in my way and was observant enough to see that the fellows face (clean-shaven) and body language (non-slouching) conveyed a different message. They said something else – this conflict made me want to investigate. It turned out the bag contained money not a half empty bottle of cheap wine!

If you communicate about a topic or in a manner that is contrary to the image that you portray, do not expect to be easily heard. For example, if you appear to be dressed as a bum, smell of cheap wine, and walk into a police station, and complain that someone just stole your wallet with several thousand dollars in it, the truthfulness of your statements will be suspect. If you walk in to the same police station looking like a perfect citizen and identify yourself as a Dr. Schkiendblist who is here on vacation and someone just stole you wallet with a thousand dollars in it, the truthfulness of your statement will be initially less suspect. Con men are completely aware of all this phenomena and it is their main weapon against society. It works because people so often use image versus observation in their thinking. If the image you and your group are creating is not what you want it to be you may wish to change it. But do it consciously and thoroughly.

To communicate effectively, one must start with an initial willingness to be listened to on the part of the audience. Without this initial willingness, it is hard to get an effective communication across. Image is all about creating a willingness to be listened to. It's all about creating the initial set of expected agreements on the part of the audience.

In my work as a teacher at a private college specializing in teaching "creative types" how to make money and a future for themselves, I have seen some pretty strange images sometimes! It was one of the best schools in its field too, with a very dedicated faculty and the resources to get the job done. But sometimes the students portrayed strange images! For example, people who are nearly coated in body art, piercings here, there and everywhere, etc. To think I freaked out when my own son got his ear pierced – little did I know that he was being quite conservative in his generation! In his generation. Each generation is different yet we are all members of a common society.

This image thing is all tied up in that old advice that your mother or dad told you, if you were lucky enough to have one who cared, comments like:

"You only get one chance to make a first impression."

"Never leave the house dirty."

"Clothes make the man or woman."

This is all about creating an image in the mind of the observer. Once again, this goes back to the advertising and public relations concept of "positioning."

Here is another example: there once was an automobile commercial from a certain established upscale manufacturer that was trying to appeal to a more enthusiastic driver market. For decades they were famous for cars that were described as high-powered floating living rooms (or boats) with wheels. They were, in fact a very smooth ride– in a straight line. Handling was absurdly bad and the vehicles usually had very large engines too. Think big, steel, six passenger land yachts. The commercial was trying to change the potential buyer's opinion of what this whole brand is all about. Their new model car was showing off, "dancing" with precision maneuvers around on a wooden ballroom floor to the tune of a Led Zeppelin song. This manufacturer was plainly trying to get you to think of their automobile as a quality car that is not out of place at a Country Club, but is fun to drive and can be an upscale driving enthusiast's car. This commercial sets an expectation in your mind that the car will have plenty of power and handle quite well too. It will probably also set the expectation that this is not a cheap car and don't bother the dealership unless you are well funded! "Keep the common riff raff from wasting the sales reps' time." (Please hold your head at a slightly uplifted angle when you read the previous sentence and remember to sit up straightly in your chair, and oh yeah – You only get one chance to make a first impression.) The commercial creates an image! By the way this company successfully changed its image and its products. They do still make a few land yachts but I have seen advertisements that say they make "the fastest production car in the world." Their marketing and PR and design and manufacturing were all on the same page and they have done an outstanding job of staying relevant in the marketplace.

So the question becomes generally, what kind of an image do you want your team to present? The answer largely depends on your client base. Factors like location and traditions of the businesses you are working with are important here. For example, if you wear a tie in parts of Florida you better have a good reason. A funeral or something or perhaps you are a banker. While in Washington, D.C. if you do not wear a tie you cannot be expected to be taken seriously. In Florida, if you wear a tie, people may think you look too expensive for their budget when, in fact, your pricing may be quite competitive. This is just one more thing that you might have to overcome to sell someone something. It really is almost all in the mind.

Artists are famous for dressing in an unusual fashion. If you deal in this market and you dress too staid and formally, you are probably not going to be considered artistically trustworthy. That is the image or the first reaction that comes from peoples prejudices.

So how should you and your people dress? You must observe your client on your visits and see how they are dressed, how they behave, etc. Generally you want your team to be slightly better dressed than your client – remember better is a relative word!

Image is all about creating this initial willingness to listen on the part of your publics. It is an important factor for effective communications.

Meetings

On meetings:

- Make them brief, effective, and fun

- Communicate with graphics as much as possible

- Large meetings are usually a large waste of time

- They burn man hours like a firestorm and seldom get much done

- They must be held occasionally

Depending upon the size of the project, this is your chance to observe the whole team in one place – are there any undercurrents of personnel problems or resource conflicts that need your personal attention? If people are missing, you need to know why. Remember open communication is necessary but so is order and it is your job to keep good order unless countermanded by a more senior executive (a sign of real trouble). Meetings are a rare opportunity to show your own image and shape the image of the entire team. The reason to have meetings is to try to ensure that everyone is aware of current plans and activities and that there are no hidden issues affecting the group and the project. As a PM, your main duty here is to talk a little, do make your points, and then get out of the way. See to it that everyone is heard fairly and then make up your mind about any issues that need immediate decisions. Don't forget the long term issues, but you usually do not need to be pressured into an inappropriate long term decision.

Since long meetings are such time wasters, only hold them when you must, but do hold them. Generally, a once weekly team meeting is a necessary and good idea. Of course, this all open to interpretation depending upon the size of the project, the urgency of the meeting, the availability of personnel, and other factors of the moment. Just don't hold too many, they waste too much time and wasting time makes you look foolish!

Chapter Five – Questions to Consider

1. *What are the general rules for meetings?*

2. *Why are those rules important?*

3. *What does communication have to do with image?*

4. *What is the importance of personal appearance impressions?*

5. *What can you do to make your communication more acceptable?*

6. *What are some of the results of miscommunication?*

Chapter 6

Money

> ❧ *Therefore, money is the single most critical resource. Yet you must remember that it is created by people. Those things that impact the perceptions and opinions of the source of money also impact the likelihood of getting more of it.*

From a project manager's viewpoint money is a way to get things done. These are the critical points about money:

- It functions as energy.

- It must be tightly tracked and controlled.

- Everyone will try to use it and often not for what it was intended.

- Your customer never has enough of it.

- It must be used in alignment with written contracts and letters of agreement with your customers.

- The vast majority of employees act as if it grows on trees.

Actually, most of the time your customer can get a bit more of it for the right reason.

Money can be said to be the most critical resource. Without it, all other resources, such as printer supplies, leased computers, paper, coffee supplies and even toilet paper disappear.

It is also roughly interchangeable with personnel and time. But only roughly! Money is usually a requirement for the other resources. This may not be true in every case but it is true in the majority of cases. Volunteer work can alter the rules, but even religious organizations where the personnel frequently donate their time, require money to survive and grow.

Therefore, money is the single most critical resource. Yet, you must remember that it is created by people. Those things that impact the perceptions and opinions of the source of money also impact the likelihood of getting more of it. For example, most sales representatives won't effectively sell products of which they have a low opinion.

Income creation is really a combination of effective delivery of goods and services, handling the various PR elements relating to the delivery, customers, and management, and just communicating with people until they pay their bills. This is so true that if one messes up either the delivery of the goods and services or the PR of an activity, the continued flow of money into the activity is at risk. If both are messed up, then it is pretty much guaranteed that the money is going to dry up unless something miraculous is done very fast. Miracles can be pretty hard for humans to pull off too! Now and again we do it but it is not good to count on them!

Now is the time to get into the technical details on the subject of money and project management. Projects have what is called a burn rate. A burn rate is a rate of consumption of project dollars. Just as a driver uses a certain amount of energy to drive to and from work each day, a project burns a certain amount of money each day.

A project starts with a certain amount of funds and those are consumed, each and every day, piece by piece, until they are all gone. Hopefully, the project will be accomplished before the project funding is used up. If not, you are in trouble, big time! Just as a driver can run out of gas on the way to work, your project can run out of money before it is completed. This is why both the burn rate and the total amount of money consumed must be closely and accurately tracked.

This is also why a Statement of Work (an agreement that describes exactly what work is to be done at what cost) must be well managed. If the accomplishment of the Statement of Work (SOW) is not well managed then you can end up not having the energy to produce any of the promised deliverables! A Statement of Work will be discussed in more detail later.

This concept of a rate of burn comes in many different colors and is really the province of cost accountants but a Project Manager needs to understand two basic concepts thoroughly. These concepts are summarized in the terms "burdened rate" and "multiplier." The term "burdened rate" is the concept of something carrying a load – envision a donkey carrying a load. It is burdened and the larger the burden the more energy must be burned every step the donkey takes.

Now consider what money it takes to run a consulting company. There are many expenses, "direct personnel" (those directly chargeable to a contract), these are the engineers, architects, clerks and managers working on the project. The other main category of costs are "indirect" costs which includes "indirect personnel", such as senior executives, and headquarters administrative personnel. These costs are not directly chargeable to a contract but these costs must be recovered somehow. More examples include electricity, telephones, computers, the water bill, rent, etc. Basically, everything it takes to make a company run. All of these things must be paid for. Perhaps it is not obvious to some but these costs are paid for by customers in the rates they pay for services.

For example, assume that Joe is a contractor who earns twenty dollars per hour. So Joe makes about 35,200 a year based upon a 1760 hour work year. If Joe is serving customers for hire (billable) all 1760 hours of a year that portion of overhead costs that can be assigned to Joe will be spread out over every hour Joe works. This results in Joe's customers being charged one heck of a lot more then the twenty dollars per hour that Joe makes personally. All of these various costs are combines into a common factor called a multiplier. The multiplier is the number that is multiplied with Joe's hourly rate to give the fully burdened rate.

For example, if Joe's company has a multiplier of 2.0 then Joe (who is paid 20 dollars per hour) would be charged out to a customer at forty dollars per hour. If Joe's company had a multiplier of 1.5 then Joe would be charged out to a customer at thirty dollars per hour.

Multipliers normally run between 1.5 (very low indeed – this implies little benefits for the employees and thus probably not top notch personnel and low profit margin) all the way to about 2.5. Occasionally one hears of a company that was running a 2.8 but companies with these high multipliers don't last long as they get too expensive to compete – unless they have some very special skill or ability that puts them into a noncompetitive market space. For example, consultants who put out oil well fires can charge some very steep rates! The multiplier directly impacts the burn rate and thus, the minimum price that can be bid on a job or a contract modification - pretty important stuff.

This is not a text on cost accounting but hopefully you get the general idea. Normally, you as a project manager, will not be called upon to calculate a multiplier but you should know the burn rate of every project/contract you manage like you know your own name. This information is used everyday to manage contracts with customers, schedules, deadlines, and personnel. You really need to know what is going on here. It impacts everything from completion dates to raises.

Chapter 6 – Questions to Consider

1. How should a project manager think about money?

2. What is a multiplier?

3. What is meant by "burdened rate"?

4. Why is it important for a project manager to understand money flows on a project?

5. Give five examples of how a project manager could make a mistake if he or she does not understand the concept of a burdened rate?

Chapter 7

Time

  Of the thousands of things that a project manager can do at any particular moment, the question is what should they do? The answer to this has become quite simple. They need to take the action that most contributes to accomplishing the purpose of project management.

Time. The purpose of a clock is to provide regulation and observable measurements to the flow of time. A clock provides a point of agreement. We can all agree that it is now exactly 9:06ᴀᴍ. Thus, project time is also observable and measurable. Without some such point of agreement, time would be an entirely relative phenomena. As a project manager, what one is interested in most is the flow of time and what happens over time. One is particularly interested in the rate of consumption of project resources versus the rate of production towards the project's goals. The element of time in relation to consumption of resources can be reviewed in the chapter on money.

There are other things about time that a successful project manager is interested in. Perhaps it would be most accurate to say that successful project managers are acutely aware of *timing*. Timing is all about the relationship of when one thing happens relative to when another thing happens. Timing how different events and activities correlate with one another is a critical aspect of human existence. For example, one does not normally expect to go out with one's friends and leave one's spouse at home on the night of the wedding anniversary, at least not without an extensive period of marital torture or perhaps divorce.

Many project managers make the following mistake. They let the clock and calendar run the contract. That is both lazy and inefficient. You are paid to run the contract. You are not paid to watch the calendar and keep track of man-hours. Obviously, that is one of your duties but really, you are trying to accomplish our old friend – the Purpose of Project Management.

Thus, time is a relative commodity to a decent project manager. Relative means being judged or measured in comparison to something else. So ... relative to what? Relative to project deliverables, relative to available funding, relative to the burn rate of the project, relative to the project schedule, and finally, relative to the purpose of project management.

The purpose of project management is to manage the creation of the perceptions related to a project as well as to manage the creation of the deliverables of a project

So how does timing work with the purpose? Earlier it was stated that project management is not very hard if one puts attention on the right thing at the right time. Once again, timing is critically important. Of the thousands of things that a project manager can do at any particular moment, the question is what *should* they do? The answer to this has become quite simple. They need to take the action that most contributes to accomplishing the purpose of project management.

That may be working on a personnel issue, it may be updating a project schedule, it may be updating a spreadsheet, it may be attending a meeting, it may be having lunch with the customer project manager, it may even be taking some time off (just possible but highly unlikely!)

There are far too many possibilities to try to detail every situation but use the Purpose of the Project Management as your guide and the project schedule will run along okay and the budget will be okay. and the project will be profitable and the customer satisfaction will be outstanding! The myriad of details that a Project Manager must track, must be tracked to accomplish the Purpose of the Project Management. They don't need to be tracked for any other reason.

So even though the original project schedule is falling behind – yawn - so what? – We have a contract modification coming tomorrow for an extension and an increase in scope of work and a new schedule. Of course, that project modification document better be real and arrive! But that is part of your business, making that really happen. If you have any doubt at all that it will arrive, you must keep to the original schedule and manage to it! All tasks and timing are relative to the purpose of project management. Just accomplish that and you are succeeding.

Chapter Seven – Questions to Consider

1. What factor, relative to time, is most important to a project manager?

2. What does this chapter have to do with the dual natured purpose of project management?

3. Why is time a relative commodity to a project manager?

4. Should a project manager look at time as a static thing that guides the project or in some other way? Why?

5. What is meant by the idea that timing is more important than time?

Chapter 8

Widgets

Sometimes things work great in a lab but break in the field because installation does not go as expected. Perhaps a mechanic had to use more pressure than expected and this created some surprising, non obvious internal fracture in a device resulting in failure. In the real world, stuff happens. Part of your job is planning how to deal with this stuff.

Widgets. This is a simple all purpose word that means all of the "stuff" related to a project. Stuff can be any thing: computers, two-way radios, even remote control cars. Whatever might be associated with getting the project done. Some of the problems associated with managing widgets include inventories, tracking, shrinkage, break-fix, replacement, manuals/CDs/DVDs and, if you will, the "right to play."

What is really amazing is how much managing the stuff of a project can become a personnel issue. People are very funny. Technical personnel can get very, very possessive about their tools. These tools enable them do their jobs. A technician is intensely interested in this. If he or she does not have adequate tools, they cannot do their job. Very often, these tools cost hundreds or thousands of dollars and are as much a part of a techies trade as a set of pans is to a professional chef, or brushes are to an artist. Thus, the control of their tools and supplies is very important.

Sometimes this can be deceiving. For example, personnel in a network cable pulling company used to get into spats over who had access to something as seemingly frivolous as a small electric model remote control "dune buggy." Cable pullers used such "toy" vehicles to pull string through ceilings. After the string is pulled they would tie cable to it and haul the cable this way. It actually worked and saved them time and us money! Not to mention it was fun and cool!!

This little "model" buggy was custom designed and built by one of the cable pulling guys. It would run upside down, had huge soft tires, big shock absorbers, and would drive over most of the stuff in a ceiling. Occasionally, it would get caught but it was amazing. The guy told me it cost him several hundred dollars to build. But it was worth it! In addition, everyone wanted to play with it and of course, one has to be careful to keep this particular tool in use as a tool. People had to practice with it before they could drive it through a ceiling...I admit to wondering if sometimes there wasn't a little too much practice going on - but what the heck, everyone was having fun and getting their work done and that, after all, is really what it is all about! People tend to be jealous of access to tools and toys. As a project manager, sometimes you need to deal with this. You need to ensure that the right people have access to the right tools, that the right tools are available, and that now and again everybody gets to play. In other words, everybody gets to share in the fun of professional growth. Or driving the funkiest remote control car anyone has ever seen!

Keeping it All under Control - Financial Control

In a strict sense, all of the control systems are based upon the basic idea of responsibility and control – particularly, financial control. There are several reasons for this, to simply protect the resources of a project and ensure that there is not a lot of "shrinkage" – a gentle word for theft or destruction of goods under one's care. Too much shrinkage can completely destroy the resource planning of a project. Usually a little doesn't really hurt but the problem is that once this petty thievery starts, it is very difficult to stop and worse, it creates mental or spiritual reactions among the thieves that lead to poor performance and alienation of project staff. This can destroy an otherwise good employee by putting him or her into a position where they feel they must hide something and therefore, not communicate as freely as they should.

Good, solid, financial control is actually a preventative measure that helps keep normally honest people, honest. To really appreciate this, you have to understand some of the pressures a personnel resource may be under. This is particularly true for a high tech personnel resource. In a sense, these comments belong in the chapter on personnel but they are important enough to the topic to say them here first.

This is one of those nasty problems that are often hidden under the sheets when they really should not be. It is a somewhat complex problem, as it is made of multiple interdependent factors, none of which are easy to talk to a client about, nor easy to get your own executives to understand and spend money on to resolve in a timely fashion. Part of this problem is that most customers do not understand the importance of lab equipment and go crazy at the idea of spending money on widgets just so engineers can test and experiment. After all the customer is paying for professional skills in the first place aren't they? It easy to understand the customer's viewpoint on this but unfortunately, this viewpoint is completely not in agreement with the real world of high tech consulting and activities. Thus, it is often hard to sell a project plan that includes enough lab equipment and lab time. That is the nasty problem that can lead to staff borrowing/stealing equipment when the same person would never even consider stealing a candy bar.

A person, we will call him Terry, may be responsible for creating some particular behavior from a piece of equipment. Often, this equipment is new or recently upgraded. The personnel resource, Terry, may have had little or no training on the equipment but is still responsible for it and for using it properly. You can generally count on decent people for the following:

- To strongly desire to do the job right

- To want to keep their job

- To be embarrassed or worried about telling their boss or their boss's boss about personal incompetencies.

- They are really dedicated to do whatever it takes to try to do the job.

Here is the rub. If Terry has not been trained to use something, but must use it in front of the customer tomorrow, then Terry, in an effort to accomplish one, two, three, and four above will try to beg, borrow, or steal (as necessary) the widgets required for him or her to develop enough skill to do their job. Hence, Terry becomes highly motivated to become a thief. This is totally weird but true!

Good project managers, customers, and project planners know this, of course, and should work *hard* to *not* put a person in a position where they are so stressed that they may put their normal morals on hold. But as noted earlier, it is unfortunately quite true that the majority of customers do not understand software update cycles, that new software revisions have bugs too, and that they would be *much better off* if they would spend a bit of extra money and create a lab where engineers and technicians can test software and gain familiarity of the latest releases.

If you manage with this situation in mind you will be much better off and staff morale will be better too. In any sizable implementation project it is best to have a lab where technical stuff can be tested and where staff can come and exercise their skills (or was that exorcize – get the demons out while they are learning how to do it right!)

You, as a manger, should try to set up a lending library of gear and software so that your staff can keep the latest greatest under control. This does not replace training. This is all about what will happen with the latest software or hardware release when it is plugged in…Which brings us back to controlling inventory.

Inventory Systems

If there are things to manage there had better be some system by which they are managed. This can be as simple as a sign out log or as complex as a manned parts/tool center where parts and tools are tracked on a job by job basis. Even down to the expected wear on the tool per job performed and planning when a tool should be re-calibrated or replaced. Tracking the parts used for a particular job may be vital. Sometimes, in replacement activities, the used parts are just as important as repairing what broke in the first place.

Certain parts can and should be recycled with substantial financial benefit to the re-cycler. In some situations, it may be necessary to send a collection of used parts back to their manufacturer or their representative scientists to determine why it went wrong and what can be done to prevent that failure in the future.

This is mentioned here because it is an issue of inventory control. Most people think of controlling inventory of new goods or perhaps new goods plus tools. Few think of the entire life-cycle approach to managing inventory. Yet, only after things have been exposed to the real world can they be truly evaluated for quality, fitness for purpose, and design enhancements. In some cases, capturing failure is a true benefit. It can be difficult to trace failure. The more pieces you have of what failed, the easier the job of figuring out how to fix the failure. Sometimes things work great in a lab but break in the field because installation does not go as expected. Perhaps a mechanic had to use more pressure than expected and this created some surprising, non obvious internal fracture in a device resulting in failure. In the real world, *stuff* happens. Part of your job is planning how to deal with this *stuff* and making that planning a reality.

There are several basic concepts regarding inventories that you need to understand: The single most important concept is that any inventory system is just a tracking tool.

The next most important concept is that of a perpetual inventory (sometimes called a continuous inventory). This means keeping constant track of the status of items in an inventory. Usually, this refers to the quantity of an item. For example, if you use a certain part to fix a vacuum cleaner, and you normally keep some of these on hand in the shop, each time you fix a vacuum cleaner, your shop inventory is down by one part. Perpetual inventory updates the quantity of this part on hand each and every time it is used. With an accurate perpetual inventory, a person should be able to look in a record book of some kind or a computer and know the exact quantity of a particular widget they have on hand.

The other main type of inventory is called a periodic inventory. In the case of a periodic inventory, supplies are used as they are needed and you never know how much you have on hand until the period is over. Periods can be weekly, monthly, whatever is appropriate and convenient. At the end of the period an exact count is taken that determines the quantity of a particular item in inventory. Periodic inventory is used less frequently today than it used to be. Periodic inventory methods often require that you have more than just enough of a given product on hand, more must be purchased and held for utilization than with other inventory methods. This holding of more than is needed can cost a great deal of money over time.

Today, many companies practice what is called Just in Time inventory management (JIT). With JIT, the item arrives very close in time to when it is needed. JIT is a great idea in some ways as the cost of carrying inventory is reduced to an absolute minimum and this can save a lot of production cost and possibly the cost of borrowing money, which in turn can make your company more competitive. On the other hand, if the delivery mechanism breaks, your production can be stopped. For example, say the UPS truck on the way to your furniture factory with the can of stain you need gets a flat tire. While the UPS truck's flat tire is fixed the factory may have to stop production. In most cases that is running it far too close!

The next piece of the inventory puzzle is the concept called Economic Order Quantity abbreviated EOQ. This concept includes knowing the cheapest possible way to order a component and comparing that with the costs of holding more than enough of that component in your shop inventory versus running out of it. The basic goal is to order as much as you need of something as economically as possible but to never quite run out. This allows a business to take advantage of things like bulk purchase discounts and bulk shipping rates; however, any analysis must include potential offsetting costs such as the costs of handling and storing massive shipments of inventory or running out of supply. Costs should include not being able to satisfy customers. This is very expensive and a very bad thing!

We will briefly discuss the basic equation of economic order quantity after some further definition of terms:

R - Reorder point – the quantity below which an order for a particular item is to be made. For example, if there are less than eight (8) cans of a particular type of paint on the shelf, five (5) more are to be re-ordered. In this instance, eight (8) is the reorder point (R).

Economic Order Quantity EOQ – the best possible amount to order for the way this organization works. In this example, five (5) is the Economic order quantity (EOQ).

OH – the amount you have on hand of some particular item.

This is the basic relationship:

If OH $<$ R then order the EOQ amount, five (5) in this example.

In plain language: If the on-hand quantity (OH) is less than the re-order point (R), then create an order for more of the widgets in the specific amount of the Economic Order Quantity (EOQ). Of course, coming to understand what R above should be (the reorder point) can be an interesting process and may take some intelligent guesses from experienced personnel and careful mathematical analysis.

Logs and Security

Probably the most basic and easily used tool for controlling the shop goods inventory (material used in a repair or other facility) is one of the oldest management tools in existence. The log – sheets of paper bound together in a book.

Today, tracking is often accomplished with a computer based system. Logs of various types are such powerful tools of control that they are one of the most important parts of high tech security and investigations. A proper log entry records the truth and that is that. Who took what, when, and why? Who returned it, when, and what kind of shape was it in when returned. If it was not returned, where is the written receipt or its equivalent that shows where it went and whose responsibility it is now. Even in this high tech age, logs are still of great use. In fact, they are probably used more now than ever. Computer systems keep many logs of what is going on inside of them and network devices do the same.

The final piece to this puzzle directly involves the Access aspect of security. Access is one of the cornerstones of security. If people can't get at it they can't steal it. Of course, they can't use it either. As noted earlier, this can usually be handled by some sort of supervised check-in and check-out system. Sometimes constant supervision of inventory is not possible due to manpower cost factors. Even in these situations, a lot can be done by building a secured area, often called a cage, in a secured facility. This stops most access. What about pilfering by those who do have access; or keys that get stolen and replaced etc.?

The simplest and most workable security feature I have ever been able to find is a combination lock where the combination is changed at least once weekly. Certainly, there are such things as lock cutters but when people start cutting off locks, particularly in a limited access facility, it is time to call the police. In the case of a contract with government agencies where supplies are being stolen, state or federal investigative agencies can become involved along with such players as the various Department of Defense investigative agencies. Pilfering can get pretty serious, pretty fast if it is not controlled. It is far better to train your personnel aggressively, make lab space available, and provide sufficient widgets so people can take them home and practice with them. If you create an environment that leads to ease of learning and hands on experience, you are actually creating an environment where stealing is much less likely to occur. Your personnel will be most likely be happier too.

Chapter Eight – Questions to Consider

1. *What are widgets?*

2. *What is a periodic inventory system?*

3. *What is a perpetual inventory system?*

4. *How are honest engineers encouraged to behave in unusual ways?*

5. *What is a reorder point?*

6. *What is an economic order quantity?*

7. *How are Logs useful?*

Chapter 9

Personnel

∾ Hiring a person and just throwing them into a project is very inefficient. This has been done – some managers seem to just expect that new employees will just figure out the project, meet the right people, say the right thing, etc. all by themselves. This is an absolute recipe for disaster.

This is one of the more important topics in all of project management. It may not seem so at first glance to you. It may seem a matter that is strictly a problem for the Human Resources or Personnel Department. Unfortunately, that is not true. In the overwhelming number of cases, HR does not hire people for you. You will either make the final hiring selection or you will at least (even if reluctantly) approve of the people assigned to your projects.

Thus, it is your responsibility to get production out of the people in your project. It is your responsibility if the customer feels insulted. Notice the text does not say, "If someone insulted the customer;" it says, "If the customer feels insulted". People are people and sometimes strange unexpected reactions can occur to something that someone thought was obviously said in jest.

Simply put, everything is your responsibility. The single most important responsibility from your employer's perspective is to see to it that the personnel on your project produce more income than they cost! The single most important responsibility from the customer's perspective is that they receive at least the value they consider they paid for and hopefully somewhat more!

Some days you may even find yourself asking, "Now where did I leave that whip?" Frustratingly, the whip technique does not work very well in the long run. Slave labor is not famous for creating outstanding customer relations. Remember, one of our goals is outstanding customer relations. You may recall from an earlier section that one of your goals is to make it a winning game for everyone.

The customer should be benefiting from outstanding value creation, your employees should be benefiting from an outstanding management team and work environment, and your company should be benefiting from the profit and future business of a job well done.

So it is your responsibility – now what? This means that it is up to you to do or ensure that the following are done:

1. Find the personnel the project needs

2. Hire them

3. Get them oriented

4. Train them as required

5. Get them productive

6. Get them profitable

7. Help them stay trained, oriented, productive and profitable

8. Administer justice

9. See to it that they have the resources they need to do their jobs

10. Keep distractions away

11. Keep it organized

Finding personnel is often considered a part of hiring them and certainly, it is part of the hiring process. Finding people could mean little more than running an advertisement in a newspaper or some listings on an on-line job search site. You could receive literally hundreds of resumes for a particular opening. That is the easy part. Now comes the hard part: Finding the right person(s). I have personally sifted through over a hundred resumes for a single opening. After a short time, the game of looking at resumes becomes, "why shouldn't I throw this one away?" Not "why should I keep this one!" Unfortunately, when handling many resumes the task usually becomes "how many can I throw away!"

You do not have time to seriously consider more than five candidates and usually that five is limited to three candidates. It is truly rare job where there are only one or two candidates who could possibly fill the role. What you are looking for is three to five people that you think are going to be worth having on the team. People that you think will have the right skills, talents, and personality to fit into the team. You are looking for people, with the appropriate skills, who can contribute to the team chemistry and fit well into the overall effort. Once you have found that top three or so resumes it's time to start the telephone calls and do telephone interviews.

Normally, the most important characteristic a candidate can have is the ability to communicate effectively. If someone has made your final list and that person is the best communicator, they probably should be the one you hire. Usually, tasks involve team activities. Team implies communication.

Miscommunication is almost always at the source of management problems. Consider how few disagreements there would be in the world if everyone was perfectly effective in communication! Life would be a breeze. Imagine being perfectly able to send or receive any communication, effectively and harmlessly. Excellent communicators make outstanding team players. They generally accept management guidance well and accept technical instruction with a high degree of understanding!

It may not be easy to find technicians who are also excellent communicators. When you find such a person, hire them as he or she will help you create the future!

There are rare instances where one candidate's technical skills so far surpass all of the other candidates that even if he or she is not the best communicating candidate they will bring value to the team. Providing this person is capable of sharing their knowledge and can communicate to his or her technical juniors effectively then bring them on-board. If they are unwilling to share, think others are stupid, or are in some way a danger to their and other's success, find another candidate. This one will make far more trouble than their technical contributions are worth.

Interviewing

Interviewing is a challenging subject. There is a list of things that you are not allowed to ask in an interview situation. There are laws about this in the United States and in other countries too. These are marital status, religion, age, disabilities, sexual preference, and race. This list changes over time. This is the stuff HR people are paid to know. Ask for the most recent list from an HR person – paying attention to it will protect you. The obvious interview questions are skill-based questions and these can be quite useful. Skills are a very important part of the hiring process. However, you need to see how this person will respond to stress. Now is the time to get to the tough questions. Questions like:

- What was your biggest failure?

- Why are you leaving your current employer?

- Why were you fired?

- Tell me what type of work environment you don't do well in.

- What type of a manager is a problem for you?

- What are these holes in your employment history?

Use anything you can think of that will put the candidate under stress that is neither rude nor illegal. How well do they handle it? This is a reasonably fair reflection of how well they are going to handle upset customers. Then after you are done beating on them, have some other personnel interview them too. This makes other staff buy in to the new hire once they are aboard. After all, they approved of him/her didn't they? For technical staff, the ability to communicate technical information can be very important. You might have the candidate explain some piece of technical information to someone. Do they really get into communication or are they stumped and confused? This technique is particularly applicable to senior level hires who are expected to mentor more junior personnel.

Congratulations, you found the best resource. Now you have to negotiate a contract or an employment offer. This is a strange point in the process. The factors are many; here are a few examples:

- How much is someone worth on the open market?

- What are your company's guidelines? (if any)

- What will the structure of the contract with the customer allow?

Many contracts contain documented rates that cannot be changed except according to the rules of the contract. For example, the rate may change according to the location of the work site, to accommodate a higher cost of living. Are there any special factors that affect the value of an individual? For example:

- Special relationships with the customer, unusual certifications or skills, higher degrees, etc.

- What benefits does your company offer?

- The potential employee's salary history and expectations.

Every project manager always wants the absolute best resources but usually you cannot afford the best of everything. Once again, that is why the ability to communicate is so important. Perhaps one or two of the best can teach several of the less educated and experienced, providing all players are good communicators.

Offers of salary need to be competitive to the market, fair to the overall team, leave room for profit, leave room for a small raise, defensible to your own management and high enough to attract the right resources. Missing the opportunity to hire the right resource because of a difference in two thousand dollars per year is not usually a good idea but it may be necessary. The numbers are important. Once you understand their impact, you will understand your limits.

Remember, profitability is expected of you. It makes no difference that your customer is overjoyed with you and your staff if your own managers see that you are losing money. If your project is not making money for your company and you are not dismissed then you have bad management. In professional projects, personnel costs can get uncontrolled and projects made unprofitable very easily. Everyone always wants more money. In some cases, part of your job is the ability to properly say no and effectively deal with the consequences.

Training and Orientation

Hiring a person and just throwing them into a project is very inefficient. This has been done – some managers seem to just expect that new employees will just figure out the project, meet the right people, say the right thing, etc. all by themselves. This is an absolute recipe for disaster.

If you take this approach, you are in no way managing the resource. You are also in betrayal of the purpose of project management. The new resource may do absolutely anything without proper orientation and training. The odds of that anything being a good thing is pretty small indeed. Optimally, orientation will take place right away… literally starting immediately upon someone walking in the door for his or her first day. The longer it is delayed the greater the likelihood that something will go wrong, making problems for a project that it does not need to have. Examples could include things like:

- Saying the wrong thing to a customer

- Violating security rules

- Messing up computer related data and programs

- Making a fool of themselves to the degree that they might want to go back to their old job where they felt comfortable.

Let the imagination run wild… There is no end to what could be done wrong and the problems this could create in certain environments. Remember that in certain high security situations people can literally be shot for crossing certain boundaries. This is not a joke. I have seen it almost happen. So know that an orientation to a new employee right away is critical.

Orientation needs to include information such as the following:

- Who the key players are and how to contact them

- What not to say

- What to say

- The layout of the building and local geography

- Where they are not allowed without escort

- Where they are not allowed, period

- Lunchroom and meal options.

- Transportation/Parking

- Work hours

- Access procedures to buildings and work areas

- Message procedures – phone numbers, important contacts, cell phone usage

- E-mail usage guidelines.

- Using medical benefits, if any.

- Location of first aid equipment.

- Expense guidelines and procedures.

- Rest room locations

There could be other factors that I have not listed here. Every project has it's own characteristics. This list is meant to get you thinking in the direction of what is important. Some elements of this list may not apply in all situations. This is a conceptual guideline not an exhaustive list.

Training

Training is all about creating the ability to produce. This ability is not easily created in a sloppy, catch-as-catch-can fashion. Sloppy training produces sloppy results. The most effective training is thorough, crisp, and demanding while effectively serving its particular educational purpose. The following are some guidelines to effective training:

Training must be an organized activity to succeed. Times need to be known in advance, access to training rooms need to be in place in advance to allow enough time to solve any technical problems that crop up before the class time itself. The technology being trained on must be in place, in other words, the phones/computers or whatever. Training is not a sales demo. In a demo situation, you can talk to an audience and their participation with the product is usually quite limited. It is just a demo. Training is one heck of a lot more than a demo. The perception of value in training is usually based upon skills gained. It takes both repetitive doing and some theoretical understanding for people get skill at something.

During training students must be able to:

1. Understand it – this means the theory of the subject and the theory of how and why to apply the subject.

2. Perform the action using the actual tool and see it work for themselves

3. Drill it over and over until the action is familiar.

If one, two and three above are accomplished, there has been a good, thorough delivery of training. The only way to enhance it any further is to use a simulation of the actual environment that students work in. Effective training leads to effective employees. The amazing thing is that ineffective training costs nearly as much as effective training. Some people have only had ineffective professional training. Thus, training has a bad name among some managers. Some consider it a waste of money. Others, knowing that their personnel are going to be in more demand after training, refuse to pay for it or pay for the follow up certification testing.

These managers hope to avoid the pressure for raises, etc. This is completely wrongheaded. You want confident and competent people on your team. There are ways around the issue of raises. For example, you could make an agreement with the employee that they will not receive a raise until they have at least six months' experience with the new technology they have been trained in. Or some similar bargain that protects the company's investment and ensures access to training for employees.

There was a poster displayed at the U.S. Department of Education in Washington, D.C. Its caption was, "If you think education is expensive try ignorance." Never have truer words been uttered. Do everything you can to encourage education and professionalism in your staff.

Getting Them into Production

If all of the above steps were put in place, then this step is surprisingly easy. Take them where they are supposed to go. Ensure their immediate manager knows they are there and will be welcoming and briefing them very quickly regarding their specific duties. Ensure they are teamed with someone who knows what is going on. Ensure they have the tools they need. Then get out of the way.

Truly it is that simple. The only real problems that can occur at this point are personality conflict issues, illness, and emergencies. But those can happen at any time and you did see to it that at least some of their teammates were in on the interviewing process right? So what do they have to complain about? As a Project Manager, you have to move on to accomplishing the dual purposes of a project manager.

Getting Them Profitable

In contract based work, you can interview in advance of contract award but hiring before contract award just creates problems for all concerned. If you followed the above program then they should be billable very quickly and profitable before too long (meaning they have recovered the cost of training them). Your main task is to see to it that they have work to do that is billable. If they do not have work to do that is billable, why did you hire them?

Keeping Them Trained, Oriented, Productive and Profitable

Quite simply let your people work and get things done. Unneeded meetings should be avoided at all costs but you still must maintain communication among your people. Today tele-presence platforms such as HipChat, Skype or Google Hang Outs can be more efficient than mandating physical presence.

Remember to use your people to help create the future! Get their help on proposals and other marketing efforts. Usually, this time cannot be charged to the client but frequently staff is willing to do a certain amount of this after hours. After all they are helping to create their own future!

If you have done everything else right, your personnel are productive. Your main jobs relative to personnel are: To keep distractions away – this idea is similar to avoiding useless meetings. Ensure that customers do not disturb your troops unnecessarily. Some of them will be primary interfaces to your customers. Obviously, they must be able to communicate freely but too many questions from a customer's employee who just needs training is really a money wasting distraction. Even your customer's project manager would want that stopped.

The customer's project manager has to be strong enough to keep his own people under control if things are going to get done as scheduled. On the other hand, if the customer's project manager wants the kind of environment where technical and production personnel can be interrupted that is OK too! Providing they are also willing to pay for the slowdown in the production of the actual widgets. Give the customer a choice. Maybe that is what they need and want. You would be hurting the value if you abruptly refused to let your technicians help users and the customer was willing to pay for it. If the customer is unwilling to pay for it then these frequent interruptions are taking your customers money and wasting it. Technical people cannot produce with constant interruptions.

See to it that they have the resources they need to do their jobs. In other words, ensure that there are no crises in supply of raw materials or tools or perhaps Internet access. These little things can amount to major frustrations for project staff and can also slow production down to a standstill. It is amazing the time that is wasted by someone trying to create some system with tools or software that is buggy but they can't download an update because of inadequate Internet access. Your job is to make it possible for them to produce, so do so. Send an employee home early if they have better Internet access there – let them utilize a cloud provider, such as Google Drive or Dropbox or a USB drive. Just do whatever it takes to make production possible. Please remember security concerns may take priority over ease of access.

Keep it organized. See to it that any managers junior to you are having their personnel working according to organized and authorized plans. By keeping everything organized and production rolling along, and the project moving, staff morale will be high. People only get frustrated when stupid things get in their way. Rules are sometimes necessary – sometimes. If you find any arbitrary rules that just get in the way of production, get rid of them. Let people be as creative as they can within their own sphere of influence and you will be amazed at the result in terms of customer service and morale.

Occasionally throw a project party. Find a way to acknowledge people for their production as often as possible. These acknowledgments can be financial or otherwise, such a gift card or tickets to a play or sporting event. Others may like a framed letter of acknowledgment for a job well done.

If you recognize good performance, you will get more of it. Obviously, you do not reward non-production. Frustratingly often, management does not take the time to use some of its strongest personnel management tools. An acknowledgment of some type can have a major impact on team moral.

The administration of salaries has a justice factor to it. See to it that performance reviews occur on time and are fair and appropriate. Make sure that you do give at least small raises to your productive people and try to give the largest raises to the most productive people. Unfortunately, most employees do not understand that a five percent raise is actually quite substantial. Some expect massive raises. This can get difficult. In rare cases it can be warranted so keep an open mind and be fair. Since every raise lowers profits, your challenge will be arguing the case for each and every raise to your management.

Hopefully, you understand that your actions in the area of personnel have major impact on the overall accomplishment of the joint goals of project management.

Chapter Nine – Questions to Consider

1. *Why is there so much information in this chapter?*

2. *What is the most difficult part about personnel management?*

3. *What types of questions should you ask in an interview and what should you avoid and why?*

4. *Whose responsibility is it that people on your team know what they are doing?*

5. *Whose responsibility is it that people on your team are profitable?*

6. *Do people always keep their salary a secret?*

7. *Is orienting a new hire to the project environment an important task?*

8. *Is a hiring mistake a minor matter?*

9. *How should a hiring mistake be handled?*

Chapter 10

Managing Your Boss

~ *Managing one's boss largely consists of giving him or her the right communication, at the right time, and in a manner that they can act upon. You should never ask your boss for a decision on an issue that is under your control. Make the decision and get on with making it all work.*

This may seem a strange topic. After all isn't your boss supposed to manage you and your team? In truth, your boss both needs and wants you to manage them. They may not even realize this if they has not been a manager themselves long enough.

Before we get into depth on this topic, a discussion of the concept of the boss's purposes will prove worthwhile. In general, senior managers are more interested in one topic than others. That topic is financial performance. It has three important components; solvency, profitability and future income.

Solvency

Solvency is a business being able to pay who and what it is supposed to pay when it is due. Your company may have earned a lot of money but most of it may still be uncollected and owed to your company by other organizations. The way accounting systems work, a company could be "profitable" but until those invoices are collected, a company may not have enough cash on hand to pay its bills. It would actually be unable to meet its financial obligations. The definition of insolvency is the inability to meet one's financial obligations. So a company can be insolvent even though from an accounting viewpoint it is "making a profit."

Profitability

Profitability means earning more income than one is expending to create the income. One can be quite solvent and be unprofitable for some period of time. For example, your company may have a large amount of cash in the bank and be able to pay all of its immediate debts but the products it is currently selling may cost more to create than the company can make when they sell the products. Thus, though the company may temporarily have a lot of cash, it is losing money over time and will eventually collapse unless it finds additional money through higher prices, investment, or loans. Additionally, as discussed earlier in this text, profit helps create the resources required for long-term survival.

Future Survival

Is the company using its resources in such a way that it is well positioned for the future? Is it investing its resources in a manner to create future demand for its products? Is it investing resources so it can meet future demand and do so in a fashion that offers an outstanding value to the market place?

Guiding Concepts

These are the three overall guiding concepts that drive a senior executive's professional life: Solvency, Profitability, and Future Survival. Other matters are important only to the degree that they impact these three factors.

So what your boss and your boss's boss care about are:

1. Are we operating in a way that makes more money than we are spending?

2. Do we have enough cash on hand to pay our bills?

3. The future - are we in a position to continue to create 1 and 2 successfully? Are there steps we can take to make us more effective at doing these fundamentals of business management?

Now, with the above three factors in mind, it is possible to start managing one's boss. These three factors provide us the guideposts to what information may be valuable to our bosses and what is a waste of one of the companies' most valuable resources – an executive's time and attention.

Managing one's boss largely consists of giving him or her the right communication, at the right time, and in a manner that they can act upon. You should never ask your boss for a decision on an issue that is under your control. Make the decision and get on with making it all work.

If you must ask for authorization, do it with a recommended plan of action. Remember you are much closer to the problem than your boss is. If you know your stuff and have managed effectively then you are probably recommending a useful path.

If your boss turns it down it is probably because they have other data that you don't have. Perhaps you want to hire a bank of telemarketers for next week's conference and the boss disapproves of this idea – and you get upset. What you may not know is that a new telephone system is scheduled for installation next week and the last thing you need is to hire folks for a job that is physically impossible for them to do.

It is actually *your* responsibility to know what is going on around your company. Even asking your boss for an authorization to hire those telemarketers when a new phone system is being implemented shows that you are not doing your job and are wasting your boss's time! You should be in communication with your co-workers well enough to know what's going on around you! You are being a project manager not a computer programmer or a mechanic. As a project manager you must communicate. Your boss may not have made it known that the new phone system was coming in and was getting ready to send out a memo about that. So sometimes this can get difficult but never rely upon anyone else to tell you what's happening around the office.

Imagine the same scenario with a different request:

> *Boss, I would like to hire the telemarketing firm, "We Call and We Close" for a one week telemarketing blitz before our big conference to ensure we get the maximum number of attendees. They will charge us XYZ dollars and I have that in my marketing budget for the project. Attached is the Purchase Order for your signature. Please sign it and get it back to me ASAP.*

> *Thanks,*

> *John at ext. 266 John@ourcompany.com*

- Now when your boss gets the memo asking for the Purchase Order he knows several things: You as a manager are doing your job to creatively fill the conference.

- You are asking for something that he can help you with.

- You already have the resources all picked out and there is no conflict with other ongoing company business.

- All it needs is his signature.

The odds are very strong that your boss is going to sign the PO and perhaps even send you an e-mail thanking you for taking the initiative on the matter. So, in this example you told your boss what he needed to know and asked for what you needed from him that he could easily do. This is a good example of managing your boss. You did not give him a problem; you gave him a reasonable and workable solution that fully works with all three of his priorities. It is in agreement with point 1 (solvency) as your advertising budget was already authorized. It helps ensure the maximum accomplishment of points 2 (profitability) and 3 (future survival) by: Helping to fill the conference—conferences have many fixed costs and comparatively low variable costs. Thus, each additional attendee tends to be quite profitable. Assuming the conference goes well, your company is well positioned to do future conferences and that helps create the future.

A different kind of example might be that one of your project personnel must take off to get some dental work. Do you need to fire off an e-mail to your boss about this? Most likely not! Unless you are already under the microscope, realistically speaking, it is probably of no consequence to the overall *solvency, profitability*, and *future* of the company.

Bothering your boss about this will probably create a worried reaction on the part of the boss. "Why did you send this e-mail?" He or she might ask. Is this employee not being present creating a problem that you need my help with? Your boss does not need to know everything that goes on.

They need to know enough to be informed about things that impact Solvency, Profitability, and the Future of the company. Of course, they want to look like they care about their staff and they probably really do, but knowing that Mike went to the dentist should not mean that they need to send Mike a get well card. It would probably scare the bejeesus out of any employee if they took half a day off and they got a get well card from their V.P. – they may begin to think they are being watched, thinking they are taking too much time off, etc. That is enough to drive some people crazy. Now, if Mike's wife just had a new baby, that is another matter altogether! It is major news! Everyone may need to pitch in a little bit extra to help Mike through some sleepless nights but that is all a part of being a team. It is a joyous occasion and should be treated as such. Senior executives enjoy good news and very much like to congratulate their staff on important personal matters or even send their condolences when appropriate.

This too, is managing the executive. Get him or her the data they need, get behind good ideas, and push. Help him or her look good to the staff and to each other and you will find that your star will be a rising one too. Your executive, if they are worth the name, can tell after some time who is really "in there" pitching and helping and who is just making noises and, worst of all, who is causing them needless worry and taking their attention off of their creation of Solvency, Profitability, and the Future.

Your Boss's Boss

This is a pretty brief topic. It can be summed up in one sentence:

Make Your Boss Look Good!

If your boss is any good and you have been managing your boss correctly you may find yourself occasionally going to lunch with your boss and his boss too. This is a good thing – enjoy the meal and the rarified company. It is a real compliment to be invited. The rules for such a situation are probably obvious: Superb manners and no touchy issues brought up by you.

If a touchy issue is brought up, keep your mouth shut and listen, listen, listen, and then say something if you really think it may help the situation or is a fresh way to look at it. These are interesting but sometimes dangerous waters. Say the right thing and doors will open. Say the wrong thing and, well, it might be a long time before you are invited to lunch again – perhaps at a new employer. At the same time don't be afraid to stand your ground, but you had better have your facts straight and be right in a way that helps the company.

Obviously be very light on the alcohol and then only if they are drinking. They cannot afford to make fools of themselves and you can afford it even less! Factually, you don't want to be around when your boss or his boss have embarrassed themselves. Some people have strange reactions when they think they have made a fool of themselves in front of you. They may think they now have to prove their power to you all over again or exhibit other strange behavior. Treat it similar to a job interview and you will probably do just fine. Don't forget the appointment. No kidding. One of the greatest disappointments of my life came when the president of my company invited me to lunch at his executive club. This was a truly upscale place where executives and politicians rub elbows—a club for the power elite in a city full of power, Washington, D.C. I blew it! I forgot to write the appointment down and was busy taking care of a customer. What a horrible thing to do. (I was not fired but it may have cost me a promotion. I wrote an email of apology, of course, and received a polite reply. But the damage was done. I was depressed for two or three weeks and felt as if I betrayed my boss, myself and my family.)

Now, what about a different situation. Your boss is not doing a very good job and you are trying hard to keep everything running well. But your boss is just mucking it up and you are invited to lunch by your boss's boss when he comes to town or something like this. You are certain your boss should be fired.

Unfortunately, you can't say all of the things you want to say in this setting. If you are directly asked questions by your boss's boss, do not lie. It is unlikely to help you to blurt out that because your boss shows up drunk half the time and he doesn't approve needed POs on time, so you can get your widgets ordered in time to get the work done per schedule. No, don't say that no matter how tempting it is. What you may not know is that your Boss's boss trusts your boss to the extreme—make trouble and you are gone before you have a chance to leave on your own terms. You are intelligent, hardworking, and professional – otherwise you would not be reading this book. You can find another job, but it is easier to do it on your own timetable rather than someone else's.

Instead, use this opportunity to get to know your Boss's boss. Gently build a relationship there. If all else fails and you must bypass your boss to get anything done, then hopefully, at least your Boss's boss will remember your sincerity, dedication, and business sense. This might protect you – but don't count on it. Still, you do have a customer and a team that is dependent upon you to deliver the goods. Do what you must.

I was invited to lunch by the president of the firm in the earlier paragraph because I refused to be stopped by stupid company bureaucracy and got the supplies I needed to get the job done and had to bypass some petty fiefdoms in the process. He very, very gently officially reprimanded me while laughing himself silly and immediately invited me to lunch at his club. He loved it! I enjoyed working for that man - he had his priorities straight.

Chapter Ten – Questions to Consider

1. *Name one mistake to never make.*

2. *How does one behave at lunch with the boss's boss?*

3. *What should a senior executive's attention be on?*

4. *How does one manage one's boss?*

Chapter 11

Managing Your People

    Managing the managers who report to you involves proper and fair administration of justice. This is one of those things that make people want to work for you and help you get things done. It is important.

If you are running a large project, the managers who report to you are some of the most important personnel on the project. Your time and meeting schedule should be budgeted to reflect this reality. The reason for this level of importance is probably obvious. The managers who report to you are the ones who will be managing the actual doing of the work and frequently, handling much of the actual customer interactions of the project. If you have failed to educate your managers in the dual headed nature of project management, you are asking for luck to be in the driver's seat.

To be successful, your managers must communicate the same philosophy of management and customer care down to the actual personnel doing the work. It is your responsibility as a project manager to ensure that they know your philosophy of project management and to communicate it throughout the project organization. If you do not do this, then the approach to work with priority and the handling of customer communications will not be in alignment among all members of your team. Such misalignment will create upset and confusion in both the customer and the project team. You will have overwork and difficulties. This is not the road to superlative project success.

PET - Performance, Education and Trust

There are three summary topics that relate to creating a good manager. These can be abbreviated as PET: Performance, Education and Trust. It is useful to explore these topics as themselves and as a series of interrelated project forces. Understanding these relationships is fairly important. Our first order of business is to provide a brief orientation to each.

Performance

Performance is something that you as a project manager, expect and demand from those sections overseen by your managers. If they are not performing properly, something is very wrong. It is not up to you to correct it. At least, not at first! It is up to you to see to it that the individual manager is aware that his or her section is not performing. If that fixes things, you are done and life goes on as usual.

If, after a relatively short time, the performance problems still exist, you need to meet privately with that manager and try to straighten him or her up. Find out what is going on and why they do not now seem capable of managing their section. Sometimes this is easy to do and sometimes it is quite difficult to do.

Often you will find that some new personnel resource was added and that was a hiring mistake; the new person is taking a very large amount of the manager's time. In this case, the answer is either fix the personnel resource fast by training them on the technology or personnel issues or just fire them and the sooner the better. Occasionally, we all make hiring mistakes – they are expensive and painful but it can and does happen no matter how hard one tries to prevent it.

If the problem is not a new project personnel, it maybe new customer personnel who is being very difficult to handle; demanding services and products far beyond the scope of efforts in the statement of work. They may possibly be creating obstructions to project progress. These problems must be documented and taken up, preferably project manager to project manager. Customer performance problems must always be handled as soon as possible.

This process of discussion is open to interpretation as projects in different companies use different terminologies. For example, the term Project Manager may have varying meanings. Some companies use the term Task Manager instead of Project Manager. One of the things a project manager must do is discover what names are given to what functions in a clients' company. Opportunities for communication failures between the PM and the customer's PM must be minimized as they can turn into a cancer that eats at the morale of both customer and service providing personnel.

Measuring Performance

Performance of project tasks is normally accomplished in units of agreed upon and realistic production goals. These units are often known as milestones. A senior manager sets performance goals with the agreement of junior managers. These must be exact and quantifiable goals. No generalities. No "make the customer happy" performance goals. Such statements are nonsense that demonstrate ignorance of managers, relative to the customer and the projects being worked on.

Real milestones might be something like, "100 users trained on the new system by the end of next month" or "50 desktop computers installed per day over the next 5 days" or "5 desktop computers installed per day over the next 5 days." The size of the milestone does not matter anywhere near as much as the "measurability" of the task and that it is an accomplishable task. Reaching a milestone is the result of accomplishing the subtasks that, together, lead to the final overall accomplishment of the milestone. Thus, you can quantify part of the measurement of your manager's performance by looking at milestones accomplished or any other similar measure such as "number of customer service requests closed satisfactorily per day."

The point is that quantifiable accomplishment must be a strong part of the performance measurement of your managers. Performance is crucial. Managers must be the most productive members of your team! Of course, their performance may not be in building the widgets being delivered to the customer, but whatever they do for their team and for customers should be outstanding.

Education

So how does one get such performance? The next corner of the PET triangle comes into use here. That corner is education. Personnel performance of any kind is usually a combination of the overall native ability of the person, increased by their education and level of experience. In the workaday world it is not up to you to concern yourself with increasing employees' native abilities as individuals. People are who they are. Like marriage, you should never hire anyone on the basis that their basic nature will change very much. It might, but it might not too, and when it will exactly happen is truly hard to predict. But you can train personnel and thereby enhance whatever native ability is present!

In other words, good training and truthful education is a bit like turbo-charging an already good engine design! You have taken an already good performer and moved her or him up into higher levels of excellence or possibly created the opportunity for excellence where before adequacy was as much as could be expected.

Good people can become great people with the right training. It is rare for average people to become great people from training but it can happen. Usually average people do improve and become real assets when properly trained and educated. Obviously, there are many theories and practices of training. This text does not attempt to discuss those in any great detail beyond saying that it should deal with the actual widgets people are expected to use and it requires theory and hands on work to be of any real use.

So, ensure that your managers are getting educated. This education can be either technical, project management, or human factor related. Do your best to ensure it is real and useful and not some theoretical stroll down a psychologist's imagination!

Part of what you are building is the self-confidence of your managers. Nothing does this as well as accomplishments. See to it that they accomplish real targets and get things done and you are making strong progress in building your staff toward excellence!

Trust

This all leads to the next part of the PET triangle. Trust, like morale, is developed through accomplishment. It is earned! A certain amount may exist at the time of hire and then it either grows or shrinks depending upon accomplishment. If it shrinks too far, a manager is fired. If it grows at some point, you are going to have to promote this guy or lose him. In the mean time, you will have a heck of a good manager who will help you accomplish projects and further your career, as well as help the entire team, and help provide outstanding value to your customers.

These three items Performance, Education, and Trust act like a rising scale triangle. They get bigger and smaller relative to the success of each side of the triangle. Quantified performance is a reflection of accomplishment. Accomplishment is aided by Education. With Performance comes Trust. With Trust comes the willingness on the part of a senior manager to invest in more training and more opportunities to accomplish and on it goes. Failure shrinks the trust side of the triangle. It is often remediable through education. Sometimes it is not. You must work with your managers and help them grow and become the best that they can be by seeing to it that they are put into positions where they can succeed. This means treating them professionally and seeing to it that distractions are removed. Distractions might include:

- Personal Money problems - help them if you can. Perhaps they can receive a performance bonus. Or cash in some vacation time.

- Personal health issues - See to it that your managers take the time to eat properly and exercise. Walks are marvelous stress relievers and are just plain good for just about everything that ails a person.

- Family issues - Perhaps they need a day or two off to get something straightened out or to put a relationship back together.

- Crazy customer situations where they are in over their heads because of customer actions. Help them through it – you are earning their trust.

- Very difficult and unwilling employees or very difficult managers. Get rid of the very difficult and unwilling employees and protect good managers and employees from other managers who don't know what they are doing.

These are just some examples. The concept is what is important. Help your managers grow and one day you may be working for one of them. It will be their turn to help you.

If you have been successful in applying other material in this book, you will seldom need to do anything more with your manager's personnel then hand them awards and paychecks. However, if there have been problems or there is a personnel resource who has a conflict with his manager then you must hear this out in a just and fair way. Occasionally, even the best people do make mistakes. Being unjust in your response, such as incorrectly punishing a person for a problem he or she did not create is a horrible thing to do; it will destroy morale and motivation like a fire. You must always ensure that all actions taken in any area you control are as just as they can be - given that you are in a business situation that must make a profit. Proper and fair administration of justice is one of those things that make people want to work for you and help you get things done – it is important.

If an employee does not think his raise or review was fair, your door must be open. But do not do this as a bypass of your managers. Doing so will destroy the trust you have been working to build up and will be an injustice to your manager. Your manager should be the one who brings an injustice that was done to his people to your attention. The actual personnel involved may or may not be present. But they have the right to be present in any matter of justice. You are dedicated to making a profit but to accomplish this lofty goal of superb project management you must be extremely fair in all actions regarding employee awards, compensation, promotions, firing etc. Beyond this, you should have little business with your down line managers' personnel other than at meetings. *Do not bypass* your managers! Never countermand one of their orders unless they are in big trouble already and you must get in there and fix up the mess yourself.

If Joe comes up to you and says, "John is sending us down the wrong path," or something to that effect, then ask Joe if he has discussed this with his manager yet. If he has, then you should probably note that there are disagreements with management policy in this part of the project. Too much of that, and something is definitely wrong as this, too, can destroy morale and team spirit. You may have to gently bring this conversation to your manager's attention. This would normally be done in private. Let your manager know that you want no harm done to Joe for having discussed the situation with you and that you are curious about the situation and that is all. This kind of situation often comes about due to a miscommunication between Joe and his manager.

Another main cause is your manager missing an opportunity that a given employee thinks is quite real. Ask your manager to have the employee write the situation down in a confidential memo to you that will be read and initialed by the manager. If the employee truly believes there is an opportunity present and is a decent employee he or she will write it down. Then you must read it and act appropriately. Ignoring the memo is both rude and unjust.

If you think the memo is plain wrong then you put it in writing and send it back to your resource or better still, tell them why in person. Do not tell them they are an idiot; rather, thank them for communicating the current business situation or whatever applies.

Employees talk to one another all the time! Your response must be fair and for the greatest overall good of the customer, project, your company, and its employees. An employee who cares enough and is involved enough to come up with an idea or wants something to change in his workplace is a valuable employee. That is the kind you want. You don't want apathetic personnel. They are much more dangerous than they seem. In today's world, embracing change (as difficult as it may be to do sometimes) can be a crucial business practice. If the change makes sense, then do it. Always do test projects at first, of course. Remember, there would be no projects without the need for change. Make the most of each opportunity and the sky is the limit. Ignoring opportunities because they are inconvenient is both lazy and stupid.

Pushing your orders in will create massive confusion on the part of employees, undermine their confidence in their manager and undermine the manager's confidence in self. Bypassing managers is shooting oneself in the foot. Have compassion and a great deal of respect and appreciation for your down-line manager's employees but never bypass your manager by countermanding their orders or forcing your own orders into a project area unless you already know the manager of that area is in major trouble.

Chapter Eleven – Questions to Consider

1. Is a hiring mistake a minor matter?

2. How should a hiring mistake be handled?

3. Why is managing your managers properly so important?

4. What is a rising scale triangle?

5. What does PET mean?

6. How do you feel when you know you have earned a person's trust?

7. How do you feel about the person whose trust you have earned?

8. Name some examples of injustice in the workplace.

9. What does injustice do to personal motivation?

10. Why is injustice so dangerous to a team?

11. What would happen if a person unfamiliar with a complex machine tried to run it?

12. Why should one avoid bypassing one's manager?

Chapter 12

Managing Your Customer's People

∾ *This should not be an adversarial relationship yet some customers are, in fact, taught to make it one. Many have found it necessary to create an adversarial relationship because of past problems. This is not easy for you, as a project manager to handle. Trust takes time and energy and creativity to build.*

The project manager your customer assigns is most valuable person on your combined team. You are on his/her team too. There is a great deal that you both have in common. It is somewhat like a marriage. It will have its errors of communication and its spats but if you both really care about getting the job done, then it will get done. Like a marriage if you put too much attention on the spats and not enough on the goals and accomplishments, then soon all you have is spats and no more project. Again, like a marriage, you both have difficult jobs, like a marriage it is good to celebrate together and be frustrated together. In the ideal relationship, you must support each other in every way possible and make each other look good to each other's bosses. You owe a debt of loyalty to your customer project manager and him or her to you, second only to the loyalty they owe to their own company. This should not be an adversarial relationship; yet some customers are taught to make it one. Many have found it necessary to create an adversarial relationship because of past problems. This is not easy for you, as a project manager, to handle. Trust takes time and energy and creativity to build. But if you follow the advices given in this text, trust will be built. It is as natural and pleasant as the sun shining through a window in the morning.

Normally, substantial projects involve contribution from the customer's side. Perhaps it's getting the security guys to the first meeting. Or accepting delivery of gear and keeping it safe before the working personnel arrive, or pushing contract modifications through legal in a timely manner. Or perhaps, seeing to it that customer supplied personnel are really doing their work; so your team can get to the work it needs to do, on time.

This is why it is marriage-like. Both partners must hold up their responsibilities or the whole thing will not work. And, like a marriage, both of you will, at some time or another, provide assistance for the other when he or she makes a mistake or has a problem. It is the response to this situation that will test the strength of the trust you have built. Just as marriages can be affected by in-laws telling lies about the partners, so can project manager to project manager relationships be impacted by rumors from people who have either an evil intent or are just misinformed. Either way, it is a difficult situation.

If this seems like a bunch of overly romantic, inappropriate drivel then you probably have not recognized the level of commitment it takes to become a superlative project manager. Certainly, a project can be managed without this level of commitment, but it will not be superlative. Great accomplishments only happen with great levels of dedication. That is why the marriage comparison works so well. The dedication to make a marriage work at times may appear infinite; and at times the dedication required to create a winning project may also appear infinite. If you work together, the stressful times pass. The key to this whole thing is developing an honest, truthful and trusting relationship with your customer's PM. This is something that must be created and earned by being as forthright and honest as you can be. One does this while still keeping the dual purposes of the project manager in mind - always working towards "goodness" and accomplishment for the project. Don't let the apparently sentimental nature of the analogy fool you. This is a business relationship that is about production, money, profit, and accomplishment! It's just that you are in this battle together and given the reality of the state of people and technology today, there are bound to be problems. It is how the problems are handled that makes the difference!

You must be able to walk up to the customer's PM and tell him that one of his staff, "Edward Creamcheese," is a total disaster and you need his side to get replaced right away as the delays Mr. Creamcheese is introducing into the project are costing the team critical resources of time and money or creating other problems. Of course, this kind of conversation is best done behind closed doors. It is not up to you what is done with Mr. Creamcheese, you just want the project to run well. That is all. This is not about character assassination and do not fall into that trap. For all you know, Mr. Creamcheese could be a Medal of Honor recipient and lately the bullets that could not be removed from his back have been hurting him badly; so never play the dangerous game of character assassination with your customer's PM. Always take and stay on the high moral road; in the end it will protect you!

In other sections, we discussed project costs, and funding. It is important to note that your customer PM may or may not understand these things. It will be helpful if your customer PM understands these concepts. At the right time you may find it a wise thing to do to explore their understanding of these concepts. One can see such a variety of understandings and viewpoints on profit and money that the matter can become bewildering! When discussing such matters always remember the dual nature of the purpose of a project manager.

It may be completely necessary to teach your customer PM simple cost accounting concepts. He or she may have never been educated in concepts like burn rates etc. Contrary to some opinions, ignorance is seldom to your advantage. If the customer PM is asking for the sun, moon, and stars, and can't understand why you can't deliver these, he or she may well not understand the costs of doing business. Find a way to educate and you may have a friend for life.

If the customer wants the sun, moon, and stars and already understands the financial relationships impacting project management, then he or she is either a thief or their company is in some kind of trouble. You must sort this out and do the appropriate thing. Normally a customer PM wants the project to work as much or more than you do! If you start as allies, then stay that way! If you try to cheat your customer, you will eventually be caught. If you have created a high trust relationship and throw it away to make several hundred dollars more profit, you do not understand the value of a relationship or you are stupid and will eventually get what you deserve.

Finally, understand that a big part of a customer's PM's job is cost control just as it is a big part of your job! You both must have the numbers correct and the same with no variance. This takes work, persistence, attention to detail, and dedication. It is amazing how easily the numbers can go astray. Particularly when purchasing decisions are not clearly guided by agreed upon project priorities. Never let a junior engineer be in charge of purchasing – a junior accountant, perhaps, but not a junior engineer. The "gee wiz" factor of the latest technology is an extremely tempting lure to someone who is enthralled by technology, not by cost-efficiency directed to accomplishing a particular prioritized goal! At some point, most personnel come to understand this but it is a lot to ask of an excited engineer fresh out of school. See to it that your relationship is guided by the dual purpose nature of project management, by honesty and forthright accountability, including detailed control of the numbers. Do not let personnel and resource problems fester and you will create an outstanding trusting relationship with your customer's PM. This relationship can provide a major part of the infrastructure on which a project succeeds.

Your Customer's Project Manager's Boss

Your relationship with your customer's project manager's boss is an unusual one. Generally your goal will be to make both the customer's PM and the project look good to this individual and to be as respectful as is possible and appropriate. You will naturally look good if you can accomplish both of the above. The reason that this relationship should be created, nurtured, and maintained is generally all summarized under the heading of, "What if?"

What if the customer's PM does something strange and takes to cocaine or alcohol addiction? Your contact point's efficiency will eventually be dramatically damaged and this could easily reach an order of magnitude that will require you to do the unthinkable and ask for another customer's PM to be assigned (usually done better via your management).

This is truly a dramatic and dangerous action. It should only be done as a last resort but it may, indeed, need to be done to save a failing project. This is a dirty business at best but on rare occasions it has been done and is necessary. For this dramatic action to be handled properly, it will help quite a bit if the customer's project manager's boss already knows you somewhat and thinks reasonably highly of you and the project team. Or at least thought reasonably high of you at one time. Sometimes, people go to extreme lengths to hide a drug problem, so if this is happening, prepare for the worst - you are in a potential hurricane.

Or perhaps something else radical has happened, like a newborn child that does not yet understand the word "sleep" has entered your customer's PM's life and he or she is not working up to his or her usual standards. (They are busy doing something far more important - creating future citizens!). This situation does not call for replacement but it is going to be a challenge for the three of you to manage through together. This kind of an event is something that can crucially impact project schedule and once again it is not so much the *time* as it is the *timing*! If the two of you know an event such as a child birth may be eminent, it is a very good idea for you to see to it that the customer's PM puts a backup in place. They may only plan to be off three days but…There is an old saying, "Men make plans and G-d laughs." The child may come out with problems ranging from poor ability to sleep to things much worse that can take a substantial amount of attention away from one's job. Be prepared and the overall impact on the project will be much smaller.

The worst case scenario for having been prepared is some wasted time. If it is done right, you and the customer's PM will look really smart no matter what happens! Another important thing to remember is that the customer's PM boss is almost certainly involved in source selection and is a target of marketing efforts from your and other companies. Therefore, a positive image of your company and overall project team is important for sales and marketing purposes too. Remember, always take care of your salesperson and they will help keep you employed!

Security Management Personnel

To understand security management personnel it helps to first understand their viewpoint on the world. Basically, most concepts of security have three main factors at their root. These factors are Access, Authorization, and Accountability. Access is based upon the idea that if no one can touch it, no one can harm it. If a thief can't get into the house, he or she sure can't steal the television. Authorization is a factor after general access has been granted. Authorization is all about the ability to perform specific tasks. You may have access to a particular system but may only allowed to do certain things in that system. For example: an employee may have the authorization to read information about a person but not to update the information.

Here is another example of authorization: Perhaps you have had the experience of a company having both a black and white Laser printer and a color Laser printer. Perhaps most users normally print documents on the black and white laser printer and were not authorized to use the color Laser printer. Most users have access to the network but are not authorized to perform the specific task of sending print streams to the color Laser printer.

If someone has something like a proposal that needed the special printing of the color printer, they sent the document to one of the few people who had authorization to the color laser printer. This was all about saving money (color Laser printing is considerably more expensive than black and white) and it is a reasonable example of access in relation to authorization.

Accountability is all about being able to identify with reasonable certainty who was responsible for a particular action. Was it Joe in Sales or Mary in Accounting or Ira the engineer? If we know who came into the data center we have a pretty good idea of where to start asking questions about the cup of coffee that spilled on the electrical distribution system. Working in a secured environment is all about getting access and authorization so your people can do their jobs and about keeping everyone accountable. Security people are the folks who regulate/ monitor who has access to what. Certainly, other executives and managers have a say in this but senior managers/executives usually listen carefully to what security personnel have to say.

Security people are basically trained to think of everyone as a potential thief or bad guy. So their native and natural response (in their minds at least) is to deny all access to everyone. If no one touches anything, then everything will be safe and they will have done their jobs. This strange logic is generally the basic viewpoint of a security person and it does make a kind of sense. Of course, if no one touches anything, ever, then no work ever gets done, no production occurs, and eventually no paycheck occurs either. Unbelievably, this does not trouble some security personnel. Their job is to stop people from accessing stuff. Your job is to get the access required so your people can work and your project can create value for company! Obviously these things can seem like opposed purposes and some security personnel make it a real battle to get any work done at all and they can excuse it all by saying that they are "just doing their jobs." Yeah, right - you are really just doing the job you had ten years ago when you were carrying a rifle and guarding an ammunition stockpile. This particular security guy is still fighting some long gone war or something. This is not meant to decry all security personnel! Their work is critically important. There is evil in this world and it is substantially their responsibility to see to it that the evil does not destroy the workplace or worse! Most are taught to err on the side of safety since an error on the side of too much access can have such catastrophic results. Most organizations have their own security policies. You need to become as familiar with the operational policies as you can. Remember though, that you are unlikely to be granted access to all of the policies; some may be very sensitive.

Information Technology security people are some of the smartest people I have ever known. Frankly, many do not have the friendliest personalities but when it comes to understanding what is happening in a high tech environment they are normally superior to anyone else. They may or may not understand business very well. But they know their technology. As a project manager, you need to understand their job. Understand that it is critical. And perhaps most important of all, understand that no one can stop a project faster than an IT security professional walking into the IT Director's office and saying that your project is a security breach opening holes in their network. When I was an IT Director, if security was at threat of compromise, I took strong action awful fast. The working rule of thumb in the security arena is shut it down, and then we can talk about it. Simply put - this is *not* an area that can be casually administered in today's world. There are simply too many risks and too much opportunity for security problems to treat this area casually. This stress is part of what can make security seem hard to deal with.

Hence there needs to be a written plan that addresses security matters as part of every project. The plan should include:

- Who will need access to what

- When, including starting and ending dates and possibly times

- A realistic description of why

These are important matters and sometimes can take a lot of creative work on your part to see to it that the right access is granted at the right time. If the project has information technology components, access and appropriate levels of authorization must be granted to both physical and information resources. Obviously, access to either one alone is not adequate.

In my experience, once I appreciated the security officer's jobs, and made their lives easier by giving them written plans of who needed access to what, when, and for how long and a short description of why, security personnel appreciated me and my projects. I usually did not have many problems. But I have seen others' projects delayed or canceled because security concerns were not considered until it was too late. Ignore this information at your own risk. It is worthy of note that once you do have the security guys on your side, they can help you open many doors. They are usually well respected, if not feared, within their organizations. If one of them tells the IT Director that they were impressed by how organized your team is, the IT director is probably going to put you down on the good side of his ledger as a good person/company to have around! This, of course, helps develop follow up business.

Security personnel often hold a lot more power then is at first obvious. Remember your customer's project manager has to go through them to get anything done too. Do your best to not get on the wrong side of security, they can be some of your greatest allies, or some of your worst enemies. It is all in how you approach it. As is true with many situations in life, your attitude will normally create their response.

Your Customer's Commitments to the Team

This topic is another very important, often misunderstood and mishandled topic. Particularly among personnel who are fairly new at project management. Mishandling this single topic can effectively destroy the profitability and success of a project. It is amazing that a large percentage of project failures are actually the result of customer not keeping their word and then the project manager not responding effectively to the situation.

First things first, why do you have this task called project management? Well, there can be many contributory factors but what counts is that the hat of project manager exists because it needs to exist to get the job done. Note the job of the project manager is *not* to keep the customer happy. That is a skill that a project manager has, but it is *not* the point of his/her job, the job is to get the work done. If one is successful in accomplishing the dual purpose of project management, customers will be very happy as a natural occurrence. PR certainly has its place and perceptions do create reality, *but* if your entire goal is to keep the customer happy, I suggest that you try becoming a comedian because in the real world of project management, no one is going to be happy all of the time! Your fiduciary duty is to get the work done in the most effective way possible for all concerned. Sometimes that means telling your customer No! No! No! Do this in a way that the customer does not feel insulted. See earlier comments on relationships with customer PM and relative importance of communication skills for project managers.

So, when your customer's personnel decide to take two weeks of annual leave when they are needed most, you had better not just sit there like a lump on a log. Document the impact on costs, time of completion, and other resources and politely, yet firmly, let the impact on the project be known to the customer PM and possibly others, if required. A contract is only a contract if there are multiple parties. It is a very rare contract indeed, where the customer doesn't have any contribution at all to the final deliverable. I can't think of a single case!

You must ensure that your customers do the work they were scheduled to do in your project plan or it will not be worth the paper it is printed on. Customer commitments include things like personnel availability, place availability, (you must be able to get to the area where the work is to be done,) and availability of software, (availability of every single resource that was noted above.) At times your job becomes one of demanding that the customer gets their work done on schedule. Demand it in the nicest way possible, but demand none the less.

Do not do this to create upset; do this to demonstrate the customer's best interest. If you demonstrate, in a positive way, to the customer what will happen if they do not keep their word, you will get much more cooperation. The customer relationship will be enhanced if you do it right.

Do not, I repeat *do not* tell them their staff is lazy, incompetent, overloaded, or anything else that might suggest a fault on the part of the customer. Be careful to never even begin to suggest this. However, review the impact of time delays on a Gantt chart (a chart that graphically communicates timing and sequences of actions, covered in Chapter 17: The Tools of a Project Manager,) and show what happens to the project budget with a financial spreadsheet. Perhaps, even show up to the meeting with change orders to authorize additional funding to make up for the delays. It is essential that you do this in the right way, in a manner that does not invalidate the customer but rather says, "well, we have a problem." Something that says, "I understand that your inspector Joe is going on vacation in two weeks and we have a great many inspections to be done. Is there any way someone can take up Joe's workload while he is on his guided tour of the Himalayas and Katmandu?" You are there and discussing this as a friend and as a co-solver of the problem not as a person who is accusing the customer's side of the team of not fulfilling their responsibilities. If you do this correctly, you will get a great deal of cooperation and even thanks. It is possible that someone may be frustrated, but that is being a professional. You have to take the bad with the good.

Chapter Twelve – Questions to Consider

1. What are some examples of a customer's commitment to a project?

2. What happens to a project when a customer is unable to keep their commitments? What does this do to budgets, morale, etc?

3. What should your relationship be like with a customer's project manager? Why?

4. How does one build trust with the customer's project manager?

5. What does a good project manager do when a customer's team member is not producing?

6. Are customers ever wrong?

7. What do you do about it if a customer is wrong?

8. What should you do if a customer's project manager is not competent?

9. Are customer's security personnel your enemy or your friend? Why?

10. Why are your customers' security personnel so important?

11. What is the best way to handle your customer's security personnel?

Chapter 13

Your Teaming Partners

∾ *It is important that the subcontractor's personnel know who and what you are so if you say something to them they will know to respond in an appropriate fashion. This is particularly true in front of your client and staff.*

This section discusses the management of your partners in a project. You may run into the need for help with part of a project you have never done before. This is rather common in complex projects, in projects where you are dealing with technology that is new to you, and possibly, where a customer has asked for you to bring in a particular firm because they already trust them. A key point of this section is how one uses subcontractors to accomplish the purpose of project management. Sometimes they can give one a flexibility and access to resources that may not otherwise exist. Some of those resources include other business executives - the ones who run the subcontracting firm. It can be useful to have other experienced minds to discuss matters with. If this project is being done by contract, it is usually up to you, regarding who you will team with, but it very rarely pays to ignore a customer's wishes.

There are four main dangers in using subcontractors:

The first is that they have been known to occasionally "turn" on the senior partner (you).

Subcontractors can attack you behind your back to the customer. They can tell lies to the customer to protect their position or to cover up their mistakes. This is something like a trusted dog turning on its master and biting the hand that feeds it. The main difference is that the master knows with certainty when his or her hand is being bitten. The project manager should find the hidden influence that is compromising his project's image.

If your customer suddenly starts acting as if your company has not been performing well, for no apparent reason, subcontractor betrayal is one of the possible causes. There is a good chance someone is saying something bad about you, your team, or your project's progress to that customer.

The second danger is the financial impact this has on profitability.

As was discussed previously, in some contractual situations, your project is making money on every hour of labor. Thus, it is possible that work could be given to subcontractors that could be done by members of your own organization. This takes profit from your company and gives it to the subcontractor. This factor alone is often enough reason to "just say no" to subcontractors. They cost you profit unless you have no choice but to use them.

The third danger is the possibility of opening the door to competitors.

Even if a subcontractor does not turn on you and does their job well and professionally, they then become a potential teaming partner that other organizations could use in proposals for follow up contracts with this particular or other clients. This impact can be minimized by creating a contract with a non-competition clause as one of its main features.

Lawyers anyone... litigation anyone... a painful business model anyone... Contracts are like the locks on most doors. They keep the honest people out quite effectively. If someone really wants to break in, they will find a way. If someone really wants out of a non-compete contract bad enough, they will either find a contractual path that will allow them to compete or they will be willing to fight an extended battle in court.

A battle you may or may not win. Even if you do win, the amount of time absorbed in lawyer and court related affairs can become a burden and a danger to your real business efforts. If you lose, this has all been completely wasted. If you win the size of the reward may not cover the investment made in the fight. Executive time is quite an investment. Lawsuits are a risky business. They can be absolutely necessary but they are painful and the only people who are guaranteed to make money from them are the lawyers!

The fourth danger: subcontractor's project management skills are inadequate.

In theory, one only uses a subcontractor to strengthen his team and to make it easier to accomplish the purpose of project management. In some cases, a subcontractor will be handling the important parts of a contract. They would not be there if they did not have some special skill or relationship which was critical to the whole project.

Depending upon the size of the effort, the subcontractor may have their own project manager. If this project manager is not capable, then there is a grave risk that the subcontractor will not adequately perform their task. If you are the prime contractor, (the one legally responsible to the client for the work being done) it does you little good to go to the client and point the finger at the subcontractor. You still appear inept as it is up to you to manage your subcontractor. Normally, from the customer's perspective, if you are the prime contractor your company is legally bound to produce; your subcontractors are your problem.

These are the dangers. However, that does not discuss how one successfully uses a sub-contractor to further the purpose of the Project Management. Here are some basic rules for success:

It is important that you are in excellent communication with any subcontracting project managers and further, that you are kept well briefed so that you can take a leadership role if necessary. It is important that the subcontractor's personnel know who and what you are so if you say something to them, they will know to respond in an appropriate fashion. This is particularly true in front of your client and staff. As part of the planning phase, you should meet the personnel that the subcontractor plans to use on a particular project.

You and the subcontracting project manager must be in agreement about resources remaining available. It is a horrible thing to think that you have another X man hours available from your subcontractor only to discover that all of the hours have been used up according to the subcontractor's project manager! A war between project managers is a nasty and painful affair. Check the numbers together, find out the truth, and handle the matter appropriately.

Ensure that there are specific points of co-ordination built into the project plan for subcontractor personnel. It is very easy for Joe from company Z and Mary from company Y to not be on the same page. It is amazing how easy it is for the little things to cause major problems. Joe thought Mary backed up the data, Mary thought Joe backed up the data. The data was destroyed as part of some other process.

Who is to blame? Poor planning - that means you the Project Manager! By the way, there is a little more relevant question than who is to blame! The right question normally is, "How did this happen?" and then the correct response is to revise the operational practice so it can't happen again! Blame is useless, unless it is the same person messing up over and over again. That, obviously, requires other action.

Co-ordination is *vital*, it can be ad hoc (a telephone call by Julie to Betsy because she knows Betsy has something to do with the area being worked on). This is better than nothing, but it is far better to not rely on individuals to ask all of the right questions. It is best that specific points of co-ordination are documented and planned in advance.

The Critical Importance of your Contractors.
There are four main points on choosing sub-contractors:

Trust and Relationship

One should never do business with someone that you do not completely trust. If you do not feel comfortable with them find someone else. Period. The likelihood there is only one option is very, very small. Stay away from anyone you do not trust!

Technical Competence in this Project's Technology

You may know them and generally trust them. You may have done several projects together successfully. But do they really know this technology or do they have only some knowledge of it? If in doubt, then it may be appropriate to see to it that safeguards are built into the contract. If they back off from agreeing to those safeguards, they may not know the technology as well as it had appeared. You can say no and still be friends. On occasion, a project manager has to be very tough.

Cost

You may know them very well. They may be the acknowledged leader in a particular technology, but they are still too expensive for the job. The overall profitability and rate structure will not hold together with their normal rates. You can try to work out a "one time only" deal (possible, but low likelihood of success) or better, you can be creative and try to work out some kind of a blended rate deal. Perhaps, instead of using two or three of their senior personnel, you can use one senior person and one junior who is to be closely supervised by the senior. Perhaps, one of your personnel who have interest and experience in this technology can be assigned to work under the tutelage of one of their senior people. This has the desirable advantage of technology transfer as well as keeping the rate structure together. Get creative - you never know what can be worked out until you try. Further, if you try to work the finances out and it just will not work, both parties know that an honest effort was made to continue business relationships and that leaves the door wide open to future relationships. If you don't even try to work it out, both sides may start to wonder if the other really cares to do business at all. This tends to close the door on future opportunities for all concerned — not good for business.

Managerial Competence

There is only one thing that is more dangerous than technical incompetence and that is managerial incompetence. If their management is not capable of having the resources available as scheduled and coordinated, that is a major problem and it will impact the project schedule in a variety of ways. Further, it can easily lead to other problems that affect project morale and customer relationships.

As noted previously, if funding has not been properly controlled, this can lead to disagreements and create a lack of harmony in the project. This is a management problem. Weak project managers are a major danger. Weakness of project management is discussed further in Chapter 16: the Twenty-Three Risk Factors .

Chapter Thirteen – Questions to Consider

1.   *What are some legitimate reasons to use a subcontractor?*

2.   *What are some of the dangers of using a subcontractor?*

3.   *What are the three critical things to consider when choosing a subcontractor?*

4.   *Why is it important for a subcontractor's personnel to know who you are?*

5.   *What is one of the symptoms of a subcontractor complaining to your customer behind your back?*

Chapter 14

Political Capital

∾ *One earns political capital by doing a great job and accomplishing the dual nature of the purpose of project management.*

Political capital is a strange phenomenon that amounts to others wanting to do something to help the project succeed. Political capital is a thing of tremendous value and should be generated, protected and used only when necessary. Thus, two key questions arise. How does one create political capital and what does one use it for.

The following is probably not going to go over very well to people who take their jobs too seriously ... political capital is the adult version of what children do to gather favor from their parents or grandparents. Same basic skill, just a different application. Johnny or Sarah does this or that specific thing for Mom, or Dad or Auntie. Then a week later Johnny or Sarah asks for "help" buying a new skateboard. "Well, says Auntie," the kid has been doing a good job in school and was just so attentive the other day at church, and gave me such a beautiful hand written birthday card, etc." Auntie, if she can afford it, is likely to "help" by buying the skateboard completely. As an adult, you may look at this and say to yourself, " isn't that a bit obvious?" Probably, so what, it worked - didn't it? It all comes down to being effective. If it worked, it is likely to work again.

The adult version is more like this:

Project Manager

"Boss, I need a half day of time from your senior network engineer. We are having a server problem that my guys just cannot figure out."

Boss thinks to herself,

"Hmm – they have been doing a good job with that client, the client is paying reasonably well, and I seem to recall we received a commendation from the client on some of the project work too. Maybe we can get a follow-on contract out of the client! Well I better help them if I can."

Boss says,

"I'll see if Maria can free up some time."

Project Manager

"Thanks boss, I think we are pretty well positioned for a follow on contract and I would hate to ruin it by having a blotch on our record."

Boss thinks,

"Good job there PM, protecting the follow on contract by asking for help when you need it and better still having earned the help in advance!"

Boss probably will not say that to you but that is pretty much exactly what he/she is thinking. Notice how the boss above is thinking about future income and how current delivery may impact the future income. That is what they are supposed to be doing. It was your job to ask for the help. It was your boss' job to decide if the overall project has earned\can be given the help.

This, obviously, goes well beyond the immediate financial picture. Your boss is thinking about future business concerns, you are thinking more about present concerns and the future for your clients. The boss' view should be company or industry wide. Boss has to decide where there is likely to be more money in the future. Boss is trying to decide what will make more future income and less present problem. He/She is comparing taking Maria (the Senior Network Engineer) away from her current client for half a day and "loaning her to your project" or keeping Maria where she is or on some other project.

Boss's concern is most about how to create future income. If the Boss has attention on the creation of current income than your company/project are already in trouble already. You are the one responsible for the current project and getting paid – not your boss. Thus, in normal circumstances, the best way to have access to the help you need is by doing an outstanding job on a daily basis and getting your clients to communicate that you are doing that to your own organization. That will breed respect for you and your project . Managing the creation of perceptions about your project creates this respect. Your efforts result in the client's commendation, thus the boss feels good about the possibility of future business from this client. This makes the client and your efforts worthy of the boss' investment of further resources.

One earns political capital by doing a great job and accomplishing the dual nature of the purpose of project management. One uses political capital to help one further accomplish the dual purposes of project management. This is another rising expanding spiral situation. The better you do at accomplishing the dual natured purpose, the more resources you will have available to accomplish it in the future. Political capital is like a large balance in a savings account. The more you have, the more   you can earn. Plus, when the car breaks down and you need a new transmission, you have the financial resources to get it fixed. The same idea is true with political capital. It is a resource that you should earn everyday and should only be used in emergencies. Of course, just like a bank account, if you use too much, it is gone and you have no reserves, so it must be used sparingly and only when required.

Political Capital With Your Client

Project managers must also be sensitive to the amount of political capital they have with a client. This is a separate pool of political capital than that of your own company. This pool, too, must be earned everyday and well managed for the future. You never know when someone on your team may get ill or other factors may force a short project delay from your side of the contract. This is an example of your drawing down some of your political capital because when you tell the customer's PM about it she will say something like, "Well, if it was any other contractor I would get pissed off, but you guys have been doing such a good job I guess I have to cut you some slack. Relax, it's no big deal – I'll handle my end." Do this kind of thing too many times and you will get a response something like, "Darn it – why can't you guys keep to a schedule ? My bosses are beginning to ask me questions. I am not going to take the fall for all of these delays!" If it gets to this level, you are in trouble already!

Accomplish the dual purposes of project management and you will have more than enough political capital to help you through the occasional rough spots; ignore the dual nature and your political capital reserves are likely to be rather low. There is a good chance they won't be there when you need them. Political Capital is your emergency fund or your credit card. Do not use it every day, only when you need it. Always add more to the available balance and you will have plenty when you do need it. You will be safe and effective!

Chapter Fourteen – Questions to Consider

1. *What is Political Capital?*

2. *Why is it so important?*

3. *How does one build up a reserve of political capital?*

4. *When does one use political capital?*

5. *How does one use political capital?*

Chapter 15

Legal Factors

∾ *What will not be done is just as important (if not more so) than what will be done. This is so because customers and contractors alike often read what they want to read in a contract and assume many things.*

There are a variety of legal factors that a project manager must keep in mind. Some of these are obvious, such as the contract or the agreed upon work to be done. Some are less obvious such as factors regarding relationships between staff. For example, it is illegal for a contract employee to buy a federal government employee an expensive lunch or give a gift valued above a very small amount. Cheap calendars and inexpensive baseball caps are the limit. Violate this and you could both end up in jail. Another set of laws that most PMs don't think about are laws regarding equal opportunity and the workplace.

The Work Place Environment

For example, if there is a warehouse that is normally staffed by men and some of the men have put up pictures of physically attractive women on the wall, those pictures could be a source of an Equal Opportunity complaint about the workplace. The complaint may not even come from the contractor's team but could come from the customer. Perhaps a woman in the customer's employ visits the warehouse one day and she is offended by the posters. The contractor now has two problems on their hands. Employees who need to increase their sensitivity and a lawsuit from an employee of the customer; possibly add a lawsuit against the customer caused by one of your employees – ugh! Headaches anyone?

A good PM needs to be aware of a great many business environment oriented laws and see to it that they are complied with.

It does not make a difference if it is an Occupational Health and Safety Administration (OSHA) regulation or an Equal Employment Opportunity (EEO) complaint or perhaps a Department of Labor (DOL) fair pay issue. These are all business oriented law issues that a PM should be aware of and knows how to avoid.

Obviously, similar requirements may exist for security when dealing with classified materials. There are a great many possibilities. It is up to you to familiarize yourself with appropriate regulations and "best practices" long before you get into trouble and to see to it that the appropriate work environment is created and maintained.

Statements of Work, Letters of Intention and Agreement, Project Plans

Traditionally PMs are acutely aware of contracts and statements of work. These have been covered to some degree throughout this text and are normally well discussed in traditional project management books. The essence is that statements of work set up the rules of the game. A key document is the "Statement of Work." It needs to state specifically what will be done and what will not be done. What will not be done is just as important, if not more so, than what will be done. This is because customers and contractors alike often read what they want to read in a contract and assume many things. Assumptions must be extremely thoroughly explored and documented in any statement of work. Some examples include:

- Physical access to areas and material

- Customer personnel availability

- Access to customer's networks

- Internet access

Real problems with contracts come about because of misunderstandings between the customer and contractor regarding what is to be done in the first place. Equally important is the legal incorporation of change orders into the contract. These are the addendums to the contract that change the game so everyone can win. Of course, any additional letters of agreement or understanding between the contractor and the customer must be well documented and included in the contract by reference. Included by reference means that though their text is in a separate document, it is legally added to the contract. Very often, a project plan and schedule will be incorporated by reference to a contract. Thus, it can be quite important that project plans are realistic and accurate or amended very early and as needed, throughout the project. Additionally, contracts will often include the list of goods that is to be delivered as part of the contract. As noted elsewhere, these inventory items must be well documented and controlled. It is quite common for inventory items to be included as part of a contract by reference. Similarly any agreements with vendors may well be contractual in nature and may be included by reference in the original contract with the customer or may exist as separate contracts. There is a substantial amount of information that a PM must be aware of. Remember a PM is always thinking of these things from the perspective of the dual nature of project management. Not just their impact on production but their impact on image too. In addition, a PM must consider their impact on profitability as a prime consideration.

Chapter Fifteen – Questions to Consider

1. What is a statement of work?

2. Why is it important?

3. What other documents might exist regarding a contract/project?

4. What other types of laws does a contractor need to be familiar with?

5. Why should a contractor be familiar with legal issues?

Chapter 16

The Twenty-Three Risk Factors

〜 *When you honestly access risk at a granular level and apply the appropriate risk mitigation strategies you are not likely to be surprised! A decent manager, in a project with adequate resources, and few surprises, can accomplish just about anything.*

I f there was ever a topic that was all about perception and reality this is it. Part of this is because we, as individuals, judge risk relative to our own viewpoint. Driving is a prime example. Some days I feel the need for speed. Others, because of many fourteen hour days in a row, it's all I can do to drive safely at all. What is risky for one driver on one day is not risky for the same driver on another day.

Plainly, this all a matter of viewpoint. Yet, it is just as real as death. Just as a person perceives different levels of risk on different days, so will an organization, after all, they are made up of people. Organizations go through different phases with various desires and amounts of financial reserves. Organizations are led by people and these people have different views of business and project risk depending upon how they are surviving in the environment. The more threats people perceive in the environment, the less new risk they are willing to take.

If the president of a company thinks next year may be a "bad year" with lower profits and fewer sales he or she is far less likely to take on a risky, probably costly, project than he or she might in a more favorable economic scenario. However, this comes down again to perception of risk – in this case the expected "bad year" by the executive. Probably, the executive should be thinking in terms of massive advertising campaigns and ensuring the company is delivering what the market needs and wants. But often, they stop spending money altogether and the shrinkage begins. The lesson here is that the wrong response to risk is deadly too.

So how does one handle risk in business? There are two extremes which are seldom workable. The first is to ignore it altogether. This is stupid and a person who is doing this is trusting in luck. As asked at the beginning of the book, have you won the lottery lately?

The other extreme is to see so much risk everywhere that one is afraid to take a step at all. This too, will kill a business. Nothing stays the same for long in this universe. It is either growing or shrinking. The end result of continued shrinking is you are gone. There is no such thing as a perfectly safe project. Just as you might trip, fall, and break your neck when you get out of bed in the morning, there is no such thing as a safe project. The trick is to recognize that the odds of breaking your neck first thing in the morning are very low and one must get out of bed if one intends to survive at all. Similarly, a project based organization must take some projects or it will not survive at all.

The key to judgment is the appropriate perception and estimation of risk, plus effectively mitigating risk when you should. To mitigate risk means to minimize its impact upon a project or situation. To effectively estimate risk, what must one do? The first step is perception. To perceive, it is helpful to know where to look and what to look for. You need to evaluate your projects with the following twenty three factors in mind.

1 – A New Type of Project

A project that is highly unlike anything your company has done before.

In some ways, this is a summary category. In essence, it includes any concept that has this main point – we are in unfamiliar territory. We don't really have any up to date maps and are feeling our way through it. And by the way, we are starting to run low on drinking water… Sometimes you must go forward in relative ignorance. This is very, very risky. Most business experts suggest that businesses expand at the edge of what they are doing now. The same thing is true for projects and project managers. It is easiest to manage those things that you are familiar with or those things that are similar to what you are familiar with.

Consider the following example: your company is familiar with fixing one brand of German automobile and it wants to expand. A reasonable expansion would be to start fixing other European automobiles. These cars will probably all have parts from Bosch Corporation; most of them are designed in a generally similar fashion. Certainly, there are differences but the differences are not as great as those between a full size, rear wheel drive Ford pickup truck and a high performance European sports car.

Resource Utilization

By this is meant a reasonable approximation of what it takes to get something done. Back to my Saab again. The time and resources it takes to change an alternator on an a 1963 Ford Fairlane and a 1989 Saab Turbo are practically in two different universes. The Ford was done under the shade of a tree in my front yard. Took a few hours. Great project. Relatively simple. The Saab – well – you have to literally jack the engine up out of the car to be able to change the alternator. This requires specialized tools and a mechanic who knows that this is required or a manual that explains it all very clearly. In this case, the project is extremely deceptive too. It is *almost possible* to change the alternator in that Saab without removing the engine but it just can't be done. There is not enough clearance to remove one of the required bolts by about one half of an inch. An accurate estimate of resource utilization is a major part of project planning and can be more difficult than it looks.

Riskiness of the Project Activities

When I first attempted the Saab alternator project, I did it from an eyeball assessment of the risk of the project. I consulted no one. After all, being a Virginia boy, I had changed several of these in my time. The Saab looked like the same thing really; almost—it was just at the back of the engine instead of the front. Boy, was I mistaken. I simply was a fool. I did not get any expert opinions. I just went and did it. I totally mis-estimated the riskiness of my technical approach and ended up having to pay for the tow in addition to the mechanics time.

Just for record, I still *loved* my Saab!

Customer Related Adoption Problems

The difficulty of customer adoption of the technology is the risk. An example of this comes under the category of ease of use. The more that users have to learn or change their way of operations, the more adoption problems the customer is going to have. For example, personal computers have been around in some form since the mid 1970's but most people did not even try to use them until XEROX, Microsoft, and Apple made it easier for the layperson around the mid 1990's. Suddenly you didn't have to be a computer genius just to get some work done. That was when sales really took off! Computers became much more popular because people found them easier to use. The same thing applies to the Internet itself. Many people do not realize that the Internet existed before the World Wide Web. The early Internet was not graphically oriented. To use it required knowledge of computer commands that had to be memorized and typed in. When the World Wide Web and the web browsers Internet Explorer, Chrome, Safari, and Firefox came on the scene, the Internet became easy to use and began to greatly impact people's lives. The graphical browser and the Internet is now in every pocket. Web browsers and related technologies were relatively easy to adopt. Now the

Web offers whole new paradigms from gaming to new commercial opportunities and research capabilities for anyone. This changed peoples' lives because it was easy to use! Easy to adopt with relatively little training.

Schedule Variation

This is all about how long something should take and then, how accurate our guess is. For example, if you are considering painting a house and you look it over from a distance, it looks fine. You quote fifteen hundred dollars to paint that house. You expect it will take three days work and all will be fine. Oops! A little problem comes up when you get there to do the job. There is paint that is starting to peel! This means you will have to sand and chip off the old paint before the new paint will stick. The job just went from three days to six days and your profitability went right out the window! That is a one hundred percent schedule variation. A profitability and schedule nightmare for most projects. If only one wall needed sanding, then there would have been, say a 25% schedule variation. That is a lot of variation but a whole lot less than 100% and the project would be nowhere near as worrisome.

2 – New Technology

*A project that depends upon technology that has
been on the market for less than two years.*

New Technology – oh, what wonder and what pain. The newer the technology, the higher the risk is. Sometimes by orders of magnitude!

The reasons for this may appear obvious but it is useful to delineate them individually because with the proper actions, these risks can be dramatically mitigated. The key here is acknowledging they exist and addressing the risks one at a time. Here is a list of specific risks when dealing with new technology:

- It just does not work completely.

- It does not work as the manuals state/inaccurate manuals.

- There are no manuals on certain topics.

- Technical support from the vendor is inadequate.

- It cannot really be used but your customer has fallen in love with its "features." This creates the difficult position of having to tell your customer that their dream is not going to happen. A very difficult thing!

- It works fine in the lab but when put under the strain of the real world, it does not work properly.

- It requires retraining of your personnel.

- It requires retraining of your customer's personnel.

- It is unstable and works intermittently. In this situation, it becomes very difficult to prevent the perception that your staff are inept. It can make you and your team looks incompetent inside of your own company. This attacks your personal reputation and the reputation of your staff.

Any of these problems can make it very difficult to demonstrate created value to your clients and their management structure. Plus, any of these issues can make it difficult to demonstrate value to your own management. If it is bad enough, it can lead to project cancellation and reduction in force (people getting fired) of project personnel.

New Technology Risk Mitigation

This risk can be summed up as: we are in unobserved territory, the possibility exists for you to be doing something truly unwise and not even know it—this is minimized when you are familiar with the territory. There are two important ways to mitigate these risks:

- Up front research

- Teaming and support agreements

The first factor, up front research, is all about choosing the right products and vendors for the project in the first place. Sometimes one vendor is competent in a particular area or product but not as competent in another. Thus, you must know your vendors and their strengths and weaknesses. You can learn this from the Internet and by talking with their existing clients. If a product or technology is so new that there is no track record of success with it anywhere, you are in a very risky situation. This situation may be mandated by your customer. If so, the customer must be brought to bear the majority of the risk burden or your company's return (how much money it is making compared to what it is investing) for taking the risk must be so great that your management accepts it anyway. Of course, that helps you little. In the real world, if it fails, your name is associated with the failure. It does not matter that the project involved flying to the moon using bottle rockets. Failure is probably going to hurt your reputation no matter what you do. An occasional failure is actually no big deal – it shows you had the guts to try something. Sometimes projects just cannot be done as intended – the Apple Lisa is a good example of this. The Lisa was an amazing small computer that Steve Jobs and Apple released in 1983. It was in many ways, the forerunner of Apple's famous Macintosh series. The Lisa was a wonderful vision of future computing but hardware to support it's forward looking functionality, at commercially acceptable cost and size, was just not yet available. A great many of the design ideas that were commercially expressed in the Lisa came forward into the amazingly successful Macintosh series, released in 1984. In high tech products a year can make a great difference in computer power. On the other hand, if you do make it go right, well, that will also be known. It will probably lead to a raise and more chances to risk your professional neck!

The second factor includes teaming and support agreements. These are the most effective things you can do to mitigate the risk of new technology. The original manufacturer of a technology can often be invited into an early adopter project. In fact, the original manufacturer may be looking for situations where the new technology can gain recognition.

This does not mean that you can ignore the earlier mentioned risk factors. It simply means that you may be able to get priority technical service and priority handling of any problems that come up along with superior customer service.

It may also mean that if you and the manufacture/vendor succeed in the implementation, your company (and your name) will be on the short list that the manufacturer provides to potential customers. This is not a bad place to be!

There are very few downsides to getting manufacturers and vendors involved early and often. One strong warning however: Ensure that the legal requirements are in place to protect your company from losing out on the deal or otherwise being injured by manufacturer's and vendor's involvement. Unfortunately, some sales organizations are, well, ultra aggressive (how do you say thieves without saying thieves?). By this, I mean they may steal the project wholly or cause you untold trouble in other ways. For example, a unscrupulous vendor sales rep might try to move your customer away from you to another provider of services. Thus costing you business.

3 – No Experience in the Technology

A project that depends upon technology that you
don't have any experience managing.

There are factors here that are similar to the risks of managing new technology. After all, the technology is new to you! But there are major differences. If the technology is an established technology and you or your company has simply never used this technology in depth before, it is usually relatively easy to find help. If the budget can handle it, the help can be in the form of an assistant project manager, and possibly, more staff who were hired from a successful project using the same technology. This might require the services of a personnel recruiter (head hunter) to find the right resource, but it still can be an excellent strategy for a company to grow its abilities and bring new capabilities to market. Once again, research can play a big part. As noted in a previous section you should always know as many of your competitors/

allies as possible. Perhaps you have an acquaintance or a friend who has managed such a project. Perhaps your company can offer that individual a part-time consulting agreement or something to help you write the project plan or just teach you about this new world. You may be quite surprised when you find out how willing an acquaintance would be to help you. Generally, helping makes a person feel good and is fulfilling on several levels.

The vendor or manufacturer of a technology often delivers certification training programs in management of the technology and in the technology. You can take advantage of these training programs to become familiar with the issues of implementing particular technologies.

Though there are no guarantees, these training programs are often a very effective way to gain familiarity with a product as well as some of the management issues relating to the product's implementation. In addition, vendors often have other personnel who have the specific task of helping "the channel" learn and use its products. The term channel here means the companies and organizations involved in getting technology sold and in use.

You have to explore the vendors and manufacturers in the channel to learn more about their approach to training. Finding the right people may be hard initially as organizations use various names for employees who help you learn about and deliver a technology. Terms like "technology evangelist," "channel support" and "sales engineer" are often used to indicate a person who is supposed to help disseminate technology related information. Gaining the wisdom of how to manage an implementation process is very important. It all comes down to you being aggressive and making it your business to find out. The only time this strategy is likely to fail is when your own management is unrealistic and thinks that everyone is should know everything just because they graduated with a particular degree or have some particular professional certification.

Your management should be happy that you are going to have a long lunch hour with a project manager who knows a product you are getting involved in so you can discuss some implementation stories in detail. If they expect you to implement new technology with no help, then I strongly suggest you find another company to work for, as quickly as possible. Your management is setting themselves and you up to fail. Perhaps your management is already looking for a new job! I have seen such situations.

4 – New Personnel Rush

*A project that depends upon a substantial influx of new
personnel and does so within a short time line.*

This type of project is a real test of organization and personnel skills. In some ways, such a project is easiest because you have the opportunity to set the tempo of the whole thing. This includes when new hire orientation will be and what is to be said at orientation by whom and in what way. Basically, you can set the whole set of behavioral standards, expectations of professionalism, and agreements in your new hires' minds before bad habits are created.

The bad news is that there is a lot of paper work to keep track of, many Human Resource management questions to get answered plus getting everyone settled in and productive. This is a lot of work. Yet it is also new, fun and exciting. The worst thing that usually happens here is a HR related problem like salary paperwork that does not reflect agreed upon amounts, differing understanding of vacation policies, someone misses a meeting because they are ill, their cat got declawed and it had a reaction to the medication and expired, and etc. etc. Anything might happen that can normally happen to any employee. Somehow, it just sticks out more when people are new hires. Teams and "group dynamics" are just getting sorted out in this phase. Who are team leaders and who does what best...it's really all about people getting to know each other. Occasionally, situations occur that someone decides to quit shortly after they joined. Better offer elsewhere, their former employer suddenly found more money, anything can happen. New employee attrition is to be expected but should be monitored because if it gets out of hand there is a good reason for it and you better know what it is and fix it fast. You have to be prepared to fight for personnel resources at all times.

A project that depends upon a substantial influx of new personnel and does so with a short time line is also risky because of the need to get it all organized very fast. Project startup tends to be a very inefficient time during a project. Those twenty (20) people you just hired are burning project resources at an amazing rate. Twenty (20) people means one hundred sixty (160) man hours (that's four (4) man weeks) are burned every single day! These people better get productive on their intended tasks and fast or so much money is going to be burned up during this start up phase that the project's available resource pool (meaning money) becomes smaller than it should be.

However, this is a time you can really shine in front of your customer. If you can get everyone through orientation and to work very quickly this can be very impressive to a client and makes it look like you all know why you are there and what you are doing.

Clients hate to see their money being burned up while John looks for the bathroom and Mary can't find the snack machine. It plainly inefficient.

This is like people being late for client meetings because when they go to the client's location, they could not figure out where to park. This is all incompetence and it shows a lack of orientation, planning and briefing of personnel on your part. It also tends to make the new personnel resource nervous and disoriented and makes them look and feel incompetent.

5 – Massive Personnel Retraining

A project that requires massive retraining of existing personnel.

It is interesting that massive retraining contains elements of several of the other categories. Massive retraining efforts may involve a lot of paperwork, signatures, and approvals, and legal agreements. It may involve a lot of expensive travel arrangements and negotiations. It is susceptible to problems such as people being late, having to take their pet to the vet, traffic jams, getting lost, missed flights, etc. Then, once you get people to the training facility, there is the question of effectiveness of the training. This is such a random chance thing that some executives consider it a waste of money and believe it is ineffective. Guess who the loser is – you, the project manager and your team.

As their oft unthanked and occasionally resented leader, it is up to you to see that the training is a thoroughly effective experience. You must ensure the quality of the training. There are massive differences in the effectiveness of trainers and training facilities. To be effective, the technology must be present. This means a balance of real hands-on and theoretical presentation. There must be lab time. Preferably, the exact same technology that they are using in their daily work with the same version software, same hardware, as close to the same everything as in real life as is possible. This should be a point of major emphasis and it is usually glossed over and nearly ignored. The quality of the instructor is of vital importance. Does the instructor know the material; does he or she entertain questions and make the class fun to be in while still delivering effective training?

There should be no interruptions including from portable devices of the students. There must be plenty of high quality training materials. The room must have plenty of light and yet be able to be made dark enough to see a projection screen. Technical resources need to work flawlessly. The materials should be appropriate for the audience. Vocabulary must be well defined and at a level appropriate for the students and their needs. Materials written for doctoral candidates are worse than useless to people without enough background. Customized materials are ideal but tend to get very costly. This all takes a lot more work than may be obvious at first glance so expect to pay well for a trainer and for training materials. If you plan to create your own training materials, recognize that doing so is a major project that takes much more time to do right than it seems like it should.

A word about computer based training and vocabulary. It is a useful adjunct to classroom training but cannot replace it. Technical materials are particularly sensitive to vocabulary. Words can have many meanings, sometimes even multiple technical meanings. Part of the skill of a great teacher is to sense where a particular student is in a particular subtopic, figure out what that student does not understand, and figure out what vocabulary related to that topic that the student does not understand. Get the student to understand the vocabulary and then get him or her through the hands-on sections and back to the level of the class.

I have never seen a computer program that can do this. Computer Based Training (CBT) seems to work best to help nail down, by repetition, things that students already understand or to serve as an introduction to materials. Somehow, they don't seem to take a newbie in a topic to a high level of competence. Somewhere along the line, a teacher is required to straighten out confusions or supply the supplementary information that a particular student needs. So, I am a believer in using *both* instructor led, hands-on training with the actual technology and CBT to help with items that simply need repetition.

6 – Financially Weak Vendors

A project relying upon technology from a financially weak vendor.

Financially weak vendors are very difficult to work with. They do not have the resources required to quickly fix things that go wrong, their staff's time is overbooked and tightly controlled, they have a large turnover of staff – this implies that their staff will be technically weak and not well connected within their own companies.

Some examples of checking for financial information are as simple as checking their credit rating, their Dun and Bradstreet rating, asking for bank and credit references and how many years in business.

In a financially weak organization, staff can be so concerned about their own survival that they are looking for their next job just as hard as they are working on your project.

It is not that you can't do business with them, just be aware of what you are working with and plan appropriately. I would never buy anything particularly complex or new from a vendor on its last legs.

There is a reason that a successful organization has become weak. It usually goes back to some personnel related issue or a substantial series of marketing mistakes. The safest way to deal with this type of company is to buy low margin, high volume products from them that can be serviced by anyone. Do not expect high quality service or goods. Buying brand name equipment through such a vendor will work as you have the major brand backing them up.

It is entirely possible to be surprised by such a company. It may have gone through a hard time but is basically sound. See how they perform. If the owners are available to you and are striving to be a teaming partner, then you might be developing a relationship that will carry both companies far.

Please note that I did not say small companies are bad! I said that financially weak companies are difficult. A company can be small and be in good financial condition. Size is an indicator; that is all.

Your safest bet is to buy from a medium to major player who wants you for a customer and is strong enough to deal with customer satisfaction issues without wasting a great deal of time.

7 – Vendors with Poor Customer Service

*A project relying upon technology from a vendor
with a poor record in customer service.*

A poor record of customer service is a horrible thing for a company. Customer service is one of the keys to future customers. Customer service is one of the keys to profit. Bad customer service is like a fatal, communicable disease. It may not kill you all at once but over time it will build up and the rest is unpleasant at best. Here is a small example of the kind of thing that can happen. You are trying to repair a large commercial refrigerator. You order a part for a refrigerator unit from a company with a history of poor customer service. You give yourself a little extra lead time because you know this customer hates it when you tell him it will be fixed by a given date and it is not yet fixed. The customer is demanding but they pay well, so you are happy to have them because you do good work and know your business. Since the vendor you are dealing with has shabby customer service, the part that you were shipped is late and is the wrong part! Congratulations. Now there is no way you can deliver superlative customer service since you are going to miss your deadline.

That is just the beginning. You have to wait for a Return Merchandise Authorization before you can send back the part. Oh joy, this takes another week to arrive and then you send the part by return mail and finally the vendor gets the part and then reships – guess what - the wrong part again! I have actually seen this happen. Admittedly, this horrible scenario is rare but it has happened. Anyway, it just goes downhill from here. Eventually you get the correct part and fix the refrigerator but your customer has already resolved that you did a very poor job on this effort and when the contract is up he is definitely going to remember it, etc ... It would have been worth it to spend more with a better vendor and get the right part the first time.

8 – Vendors with Executive Failures - Poor Success Rates

A project heavily involving technology from a vendor
whose executives have a poor record of success.

Executive success is a very tricky thing; business success does not come easily nor often. Most companies die in their first year. Some make it to two years, fewer still, to three. It starts to stabilize after that. So if an executive has kept a company alive for at least two years, he or she can be ranked at least somewhat successful, three years is even more successful. Longer than three years is a definite success. Business is not easy and founding a company is quite an accomplishment indeed!

A poor track record of success would be someone taking over a running concern and then running it into the ground – that is true failure! One year in business is a learning experience; two years in business is the same. Businesses fail less often after three years. After three years, an executive should pretty well know the game and unless there are major changes in business or market environment, they should be able to keep their company going and growing.

Major changes in the environment or business environment may be too much for even the best executive to handle. An example of this include the terrorist's attack on September 11th, 2001. The reaction of most companies was to stop spending almost completely. This drastically reduced many markets and killed a number of companies. This was particularly true in high tech. Another example is the travel industry immediately following the same catastrophe. A different kind of example is a tsunami which wipes out a resort area. No resort area, no sales for the business that served the resort area. Extenuating circumstances can occur that can make business failures understandable. The executives themselves are hurt badly - they often go from six figure salaries down to nothing and have to rebuild their lives, from nearly nothing. Life can be tough. Fortunately, if they can get over the disaster in their own mind, they can rebuild and try again. This is not a failed executive, this is an executive who is fighting back! Executives create the company. I have never seen a group that is more dedicated to its tasks than its executives. Executives maintain the standards and mores of the group. Failed executives have given up or worse.

If they are out partying when they should be working, the worst project staff is going to emulate them and the best staff is going to look for other work because they know the group is headed for failure. Certainly, senior executives have a duty to go to certain parties, meet at restaurants etc., but that is working. Staying up until ridiculous hours, coming in with a hangover, maintaining a drug problem – this is just unethical behavior. Leave such situations as quickly as possible. Executives who behave this way do not care about themselves, their customers, nor their staff. They may make noises about caring but look at the results of their actions, not their noises. They are simply a danger to all around them. They need to be told to straighten up by a more senior executive or shown the door and the sooner the better!

9 – Vendors with Poor Technical Success

A project relying upon technology from a vendor
who has a poor record of technical success.

If they failed technically before, and then failed technically again, and then failed technically again why should this time be any different? This does not mean that you can't check out a company with a reputation for failure. Didn't Thomas Edison say that failure was just another form of progress? It is if you learn from it. Sometimes that can be hard to do and some people don't seem too able to change so they end up out of business for good. Consider the beginning of the age of the automobile. Those carriage manufacturers that adopted themselves to automobile body work did okay., at least for a while. Those that refused to change - well, they ended up doing other things with their time.

Unless you have technical expertise in a given subject, it is risky to try to judge whether a company has learned from its technical failures or is apt to fail again. Send your best and most creative engineers to survey a company and task them with figuring out if they are willing to gamble their careers on the company that has failed technically several times. If they say yes, go check out the marketing and administrative matters yourself and if it still looks good, well, it's only your career, the home and your car ... Make up your mind with all of the data and perception you can and go forward; knowing you did the best job you could, whatever your decision!

10 – No Priority Service Agreement from the Vendor

*A project relying upon a technology from a vendor who will
not make a priority service agreement with your team.*

A priority service agreement means your needs for customer service will be put ahead of the average customer. No priority service from the vendor: a simple decision, don't use them! The last thing you want is to be treated the same way that some person who does not have a lot of money and many careers riding on how they are treated. If you can't get priority customer service agreement in writing then you don't need to use that company's technology!

11 – No Contact with Sales Rep, Engineers, and Managers

*A project involving technology from a vendor who will not let you talk,
face to face, with Sales Engineers, Sales Managers and Sales reps.*

This point of risk is less clear in today's world where everything is done via e-mail, web sites, instant messaging, and teleconference. Remaining old fashioned on this point is not a bad thing. Business runs on relationships. Relationships are built on trust. I want to see the look in the Systems Engineer's eye when he tells me the next release will fix that bug we just ran into! I want him or her to know that I am going to be giving them a piece of my mind if they lie to me. That I am serious and I will do my best to make their reputation mud if I discover that they did not fulfill their fiduciary responsibility to any project that I am managing.

12 – Management Indifference to the Project

Any project your company's management does not get enthusiastic about.

Projects that your company's management is not enthused about are very dangerous to manage. There is one highly inclusive summary description that covers most of them. It could be called weird internal politics. Within "weird internal politics" there is any number of possible sub-factors.

Note there is no permanent relative importance of these factors. They are all important at relative levels at different times. These are the factors:

- Information they won't tell you

Oh yes! There is frequently data that senior executives know, that they are not willing to impart to project management or even director level personnel. This might include situations like:

- Your Vice President is about to be fired

- The company is about to be sold

- The company is being sued and the project you are running could have something to do with it. For example, this project uses the same products or some of the same personnel, customers or partners involved in the law suit.

- Your division is about to be closed and when you are done with this project there will be a major reduction in force (you and many of others will suddenly be out of work)

- New, extremely powerful competition has entered into the arena that your executives doubt they can successfully fight

- The senior executives of the company are about to make strategic alliances that will make this project (and to some degree, you) a thing of the past.

- New technology is hitting the market that makes your project resemble a buggy whip manufacturer after people had converted from horse and buggies to automobiles for transport.

- Your second cousin upset the daughter or son of an important manager or stockholder. In other words, for no apparently sane reason whatsoever. Sometimes even good managers fail to communicate.

- You have been successful in the past and have earned several raises. You poor son of a gun, now you are expensive. Expensive is another word for easily unemployed!

Once again, these are just some examples. It makes no difference what the silly logic is. Senior executives often do not communicate as effectively as they should and, given their responsibilities to the company, it is understandable that sometimes things must be kept generally confidential. Still, lack of senior executive enthusiasm for your project is a bad sign. Once they have lost enthusiasm, you will have to work doubly hard to handle the image of the project and will have to do so with fewer resources than would have been available in a "normal" project. This is difficult but possible.

One way to look at this situation is to consider it an exchange between your delivery team and the company overhead. Is the company backing the project up? Are you getting the personnel and widgets that you need and can afford? Or is someone stonewalling the project "back at corporate." The "reasons" can range from personnel procurement expenses to someone "back at corporate" being bigoted against people with wide feet whose socks don't match their shirt! If senior execs appear to lose their enthusiasm, perhaps you need to take more initiative and pro-actively communicate with them. Their reaction to your pro-activity may tell you even more. If they are willing to communicate and seem interested, then you are probably on safe ground, at least for the time being. If they will not communicate with you, brush up that resume because you are probably going to need it within a matter of weeks.

Just do your best and deal with it. If you have been following the advices laid out in the rest of this text, your reputation is probably in pretty good shape and you may even be able to wrangle a transfer. Senior executives can keep secrets and still communicate adequate information. It is the lack of communication that should make you sweat, not the secrets!

13 – Oversold Projects

Projects that were "oversold." This is a case involving an under-managed sales rep who has set ridiculous expectations.

Well, if life wasn't challenging, you would be bored right? Customers can be pretty funny sometimes. Remember, one of the most important things you can do is to find out what the customer thinks they bought and compare that to the contract and pro-actively get the contract modified into a realistic deliverable. If this can't be done, then you have major problems on your hands and you need to write up a detailed memo on the whole situation and get it into the hands of senior executives as you update your resume! What should happen is the salesperson should be educated and perhaps disciplined and you should be a hero for preventing the company from getting stuck into a money losing deal.

What will probably happen is that the salesperson will receive a small slap on the wrist. Your reputation as being sales friendly will be damaged and you may be considering your future employment options. This is ugly but sales must rule the world or there will not be enough sales. *That* is what senior managers are interested in, sales and profit from sales! This is part of why managing the salesperson is such a critical factor in the life of a project manager. It should not have to be, but it is. Life is not fair. Get over it. Get creative, get busy communicating, and get back to work!

14 – Weak Customer Project Managers

Projects with a weak customer project manager are some of the most difficult and dangerous projects. Due to your customer project manager's weakness within his/her own company, they cannot be trusted to deliver what they promise in a timely fashion.

The overwhelming majority of organizations are not very sane. They make astounding mistakes particularly in the areas of customer service, personnel and project management. You may have noticed this yourself by now. It takes a personality with a certain amount of strength of character plus the ability to navigate through the formal policies and handle the politics of informal cliques to get something (anything!) done. Thus, in many situations, an ineffective customer project manager can be the worst thing that can happen to your project. The ineffective customer project manager will cause project delays and is fully capable of turning what should have been a reasonably profitable project, into an unprofitable mess.

Say that your team needs access to building Q to work on a project inside, and normally access to building Q is restricted. The customer's project manager was supposed to get the authorization but did not get it and never told you. Silly as this sounds, it happens with regularity. Now your team shows up and may wait around for 3 hours while the customer project manager sorts this mess out. Your team consisted of two or three people, there goes one man-day of funding right out the window with *nothing* to show for it. Expense without production impacts project schedules and may have a rippling effect. This delay may mean that other personnel cannot do their jobs. Depending upon the situation, this can cause very expensive downstream impacts.

Horrible!

Weak customer project managers should be avoided. If it is bad enough, write memos that document what has happened and perhaps request a change of customer project manager. Realize this is unlikely to make you many friends within your company or the customer's. But it may be necessary.

15 – Indifferent Customers

The customer does not care if the project gets done in a timely manner.

One could think that such a project would be easy to accomplish, as there would not be stress from the client side. However, this situation is likely to translate into a lack of cooperation from the client and it will be a fight to get more money from them to make up for their slowness and lack of dedication.

Projects that are recognized as important by client management are much easier to get done and much easier to make profitable than those where the client is not motivated.

Think of this in terms of time and money. You probably have a relatively fixed project budget. You have contract deliverables to accomplish. This does not change just because your customer does not particularly care. Your company is spending its money and resources by having you and your team on site. Your management cannot let this go on forever unless your company is paid.

The customer is very likely to forget that they have been delaying the project when it is time to pay the bills. Someone, perhaps their comptroller, will ask "why are we paying these invoices from HoBo consulting? We still don't have the files updated and they were supposed to do that a month ago! I am not paying this bill until the work is done! Period!" The comptroller does not care that you have been asking to get into the room with those files for four weeks but you cannot get access because no one cares enough to get you a key! The customer's lack of dedication and overall ineffectiveness is destroying your project's budget and therefore your project! Your management does not particularly care about why the project is taking too long, or why it is losing money. Management wants profit not losses and if they are doing their jobs, they will normally find someone who can stop losses pretty quickly if you can't. Good luck in your next position.

16 – Unbelievably Profitable Projects

Projects that appear to be unbelievably profitable. If a project appears to be unbelievably profitable it means one of a short list of things is occuring.

1. The project is very risky and you should be very aware of that and plan for it by using every risk mitigation strategy you can think of.

2. You and your company do not actually understand the real scope of the project (at least from the customer's viewpoint).

3. Your rates are way too high to stay competitive.

4. Something not in the normal realm of acceptable business practices is going on.

It may not quite be illegal, but somewhere, someone is violating or manipulating their fiduciary responsibility somehow. From the project manager position this is not an easy thing to sort out. Indeed, it may not even be your job to sort it out. But if you don't know what is going on, you are at risk. So it is strongly recommended that you ensure that the apparent profitability does not come from 1, 2, 3 or 4 above. You can even do some light investigation of 4 above but I do not encourage you to go deep here. Depending upon the size of your company there may be a business ethics committee or other such body that you can anonymously submit a memo to. That should definitely be done. If something is not right and your company is involved in it, only bad things will come of that. This is the realm of senior corporate executives, forensic auditors, and possibly the Federal Bureau of Investigation. Try to document your concerns and disentangle yourself from the mess. If you are approached by your own corporate executives in the matter, let your conscience be your guide. This is dangerous territory.

17 – Non-profitable Projects

Some projects will be very hard to make profitable.

There are many things that can cause a situation like this. Some of these factors include:

1. Costs were originally mis-estimated – can easily occur with new technology.

2. Project scope was allowed to increase without matching funding increases. This is sometimes called "scope creep." A definite sign of weak project management.

3. This is a project that the company decided to do at a loss or near loss because it gave them access to something they want very badly, such as an initial project for a particular customer where management thinks it can make a substantial profit in the future. Alternatively, management may wish to have corporate experience with new technology that they think is a strategic advantage.

4. To make up for some past project where the client was not dealt with as fairly as might have been expected. The world of business can be pretty strange sometimes. This is something like doing something extra special for one's mate because one did something not showing the best judgment recently.

5. Someone is trying to sabotage the company or at least a particular effort. This is evil and it is rare but it can happen. If you find yourself in this situation, gently try to stop the source of sabotage, as it might be accidental or due to misunderstanding. If it won't fix, document the situation and be prepared to leave as quickly as you can before your reputation becomes involved in the disaster.

Projects that appear to be very hard to make profitable are often better than they look at first glance. This is particularly true if you are coming in as the magic bullet to fix it. In this case you are in the limelight. If you succeed, it will be known that you are the *one!* On the other hand if you fail, well you may not be the *one,* this time, but then again perhaps no one could be the *one* this time. Your executives know it was a difficult situation to begin with and are not as likely to show you the door as they would be when a project manager fails at a normal project. Thus, though this type of project is very hard work for the project manager and stressful, in some ways it is a win-win for the project manager. Succeed and there is at least some glory. Fail and it's not certain death.

Senior management may have decided that losing money on this project is actually an investment in the future. Because the company will be one of the few with experience implementing some new technology that makes your company more competitive. Of course, this makes you one of the few project managers who have experience managing this new technology. This is very exciting stuff and being picked as the project manager for this category of project is a tremendous compliment to you. Once again, you are in the limelight. If your company is well managed, expect to be watched. Many people will want to know what is going on. Some people will be jealous. Apply the rules in this text about risk elimination and truly succeed. Max out your creative management juices and win, baby win. When you pull one of these off as a success it opens the door to a whole new future. Fail and, well, it's probably time to polish up the old resume again. Still, you will have exposure to some new things and if you can learn from what went wrong, you may find yourself and your experience quite valuable in the marketplace.

18 – Legal and Contract Issues

These are generally difficult and can be an invitation to difficult problems.
At times your options will be limited by legal and contractual requirements.

You face a difficult challenge if the contract calls for certain restrictions that were not considered during the pricing phase of negotiations, such as when your normal partners cannot work the job for legal reasons, or anything which breaks your successful pattern of operation. Creativity and your network of industry contacts will be your most valuable asset in this situation. You may have to do a lot of extra work, extra reports and documentation, extra customer hand holding, extra internal meetings, extra everything! Finding alternative resources can take a lot of your time as many of your normal resources are not available because of contractual restrictions.

Say there is a provider that you like to cooperate with, perhaps an electrical installer. You have developed a relationship with their management team and some of their personnel, their work quality is high, and their prices are reasonable. *However* they do not have the required bonding or security clearance for a particularly sensitive project. This means that you have to create a new relationship with a new electrical company and ensure that they meet both the contractual requirements (perhaps a very large bond) and can reliably do the work. Your challenge is to remember to accomplish the basic purpose of a project manager regardless of the resistance and problems and you will win through.

Do your best at the beginning of the project to understand exactly what the legal or contractual situation is and understand what factors led up to the situation. This may give you important background that will help you understand the real rules of the playing field up front. Trust may be hard to come by. Earn it – quickly and repeatedly. Value creation earns trust. Create your project plan with a strong emphasis on early and frequent wins and meet the milestones.

If you are taking over a project that is in trouble with threatened lawsuits, you will need to re-create the project. Trust needs to be re-created among all parties, and that can be quite a task. Developing trust when you are in the middle of a lawsuit is challenging. Still it can be done! Recall the earlier story about an east coast city that was threatening to sue a computer company over non-delivery. What was needed was the creation of a new relationship with the city's IT director using truthful, effective communication and ensuring that true value was delivered. Accomplishing the re-creation of trust led to the city attorneys being called off and major additional sales.

Project recovery is done by hard work, good and flexible planning and execution that is full of care. Care and accomplishment are key. Care breeds trust. On time accomplishments breed trust.

19 – International Projects

Projects that require cultural boundaries to be frequently crossed can be problematic, particularly if they must be managed from a great distance.

This risk factor and the two following share a very important common thread. All discuss hazards that have to do with the acceptability of communication across various cultures and various spheres of interest. Sometimes these spheres of interest are called "rice bowls," cliques, or divisions of companies, or countries. What we are dealing with here involves the curious subject called cultural anthropology. This is the study of man and his cultures and how mankind tends to break itself into groups and how these groups interact and what the traditions and the morals of particular groups are, plus what role these traditions and morals serve. Huge sentence. Man is a huge topic.

To communicate most effectively across an array of cultures, it helps to know several things bout them. Among these are:

- Who and what they fear

- Who and what they consider beneficial to their survival

- Who and what they respect most

- What they consider good

- What they consider bad or dangerous

- What a trustworthy person looks like to them

- What an untrustworthy person or criminal looks like to them

- What words have what connotations to them?

Once you wrap your mind around all of these factors you will be fairly successful in communicating. If you just start talking with total disregard to the points above, then luck is in the driver's seat. I don't like luck in the drivers seat... ever.

Now, don't misunderstand that I am saying you must perform a deep battery of ethnological/sociological/psychological tests on people before you can communicate to them. That is not the point. The point is that you need to very quickly survey the situation and find out what the sensitive topics are. If you just put attention on communicating with regard to the points above with the sales reps and other personnel who have been there, you will be much better off. You can even buy a book and read about the culture where one is getting ready to do a project. I did this when I went to China and though far from perfect, it was a great help!

A somewhat obvious example of this is holidays. Different countries have different holidays. For that matter, different cultures in the same country have different holidays. These holidays directly impact staff availability and therefore impact a project plan and a project manager.

For example, Independence Day is July 4th in the United States. The Fifth of May, Cinco de Mayo, is a celebration of Mexican American culture, however, many Americans mistakenly call it Mexico's Independence Day. Actually, this holiday commemorates the victory of the Mexican army over the French at the Battle of Puebla on May 5, 1862. In Mexico, this is a full national holiday with military parades. Both countries celebrate these national holidays with enthusiasm.

Religious holidays are another example. People of varying religions need different times off. For many Christians, Easter is critically important. The Jewish New Year and Yom Kippor are days a Jewish employee would need to take off. A Muslim employee will need to break their fast each sundown during the month of Ramadan. Sometimes cities will take a day or a week off. Try getting something done in Rio De Janeiro during Carnival! It is all about understand the culture.

One final word on this topic. I have worked on various types of projects in eleven different countries. This entire time I always went out of my way to be aware of local customs and to be humble, for I was a guest in a foreign land. Yes, I was and am a proud citizen of a very powerful nation. Does that, in some way, make me a better person then someone who has invited me into their country to help them learn or get something done? I think not! You should always feel honored when someone decides that you are worth spending their hard earned money on. When someone goes to the expense of flying you into their country and paying for your food and hotel bills you better feel very honored and very humbled. I have been told by the customer that it was my attitude that set me apart from other foreigners. I was not haughty and I helped them as I would help any employer. That does not mean that you don't use your power when you need to but it does mean that you are aware of local customs and rituals and use this awareness to your advantage! You are an honored guest–act like one. Be kind and *listen*.

20 – A Multi-Lingual Project Environment

Projects that require participants with a variety of native languages.

One of the most difficult things I have ever done was to try to understand and manage a contract that was originally written in a foreign language. Translation is not an exact science. I have heard that translators for diplomats of governments from foreign countries try to spend some time together to grow accustomed to each other's style of translation before the heads of state discuss things. If there is a misunderstanding between the translators… well, the result could be quite a difficult situation.

Like a head of state, a project manager who is managing projects which are not in their native tongue is completely at the mercy of the translator. This is not comfortable. In addition, the odds of having continuous access to a translator of extremely high skill are not high when project budgets are considered. For example, a missionary may be an excellent translator. The missionary may know how to explain the Bible in five different languages. However, in their education the conceptual understanding of business methods and technical factors were given less emphasis. Now imagine three project managers and three engineers, all trying to communicate about a weird technical problem. Particularly, when the only one (the translator) who understands everyone does not really understand technology and you are trying to manage a technology project! This is a difficult situation at best! Rule of thumb: Unless you are already an exceptional communicator, do not try to accomplish such a multi-lingual project. If you are an exceptional communicator, you must allow for substantial cost overruns and delays. Your best weapon is an outstanding translator who understands both business and the technologies you are dealing with. Such skills do not normally come cheap!

21 – Crossing the Political Divide

Projects that span many divisions of an organization.

Welcome to the wonderful world of bureaucratic politics. Whose rice bowl shall we play in today? The more divisional boundaries you cross, the more time it takes to handle politics and the impact of politics on the project plan increases. This can get quite time consuming.

The chart on the next page shows this situation:

Cost and Complexity

(chart with y-axis values: 3000, 2500, 2000, 1500, 1000, 500, 0 and x-axis values: 1 2 3 4 5 6 7 8 9 10 11)

Number of Organizational Boundaries Crossed

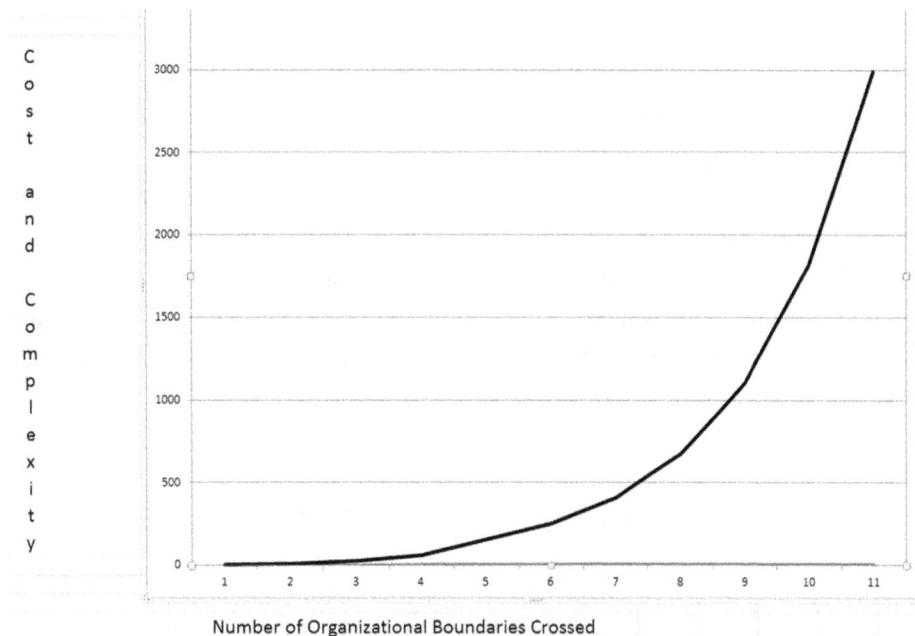

This graph has many applications; the essence of its meaning is this: If a project crosses organizational boundaries, there will be additional time and complexities introduced just by crossing the boundaries. Usually these complexities are induced by various human factors. The exact point where the curve becomes nearly vertical varies from project to project but it is out there somewhere, just waiting to be reached. It usually becomes a problem sooner rather than later.

Now for some good news! This complexity is actually an opportunity for a great project manager to shine like a star. Normally, there is a reason a project involves multiple divisions. This means that there must be value to add from each division that is crossed. Look at this situation from the perspective of the purpose of a project manager. Each division is opportunity to add value, add to your team's reputation, and increase the marketing opportunities for your company. If you run the project right this is a glorious opportunity, not a problem. Projects that span multiple divisions are like a gift from someone who loves you because of the exposure they give the project team. If your team shows its caring attitude in each division it touches and your marketing comes along at the right time ... wow, what better time to approach a potential customer than when they were just amazed by your groups' personnel? Yes, this means that you must have a real team. It means they must be able to deliver superlative service. It means that you must have a plan that includes training and communications with each and every group. That is good project management. That is the way it is supposed to be!

Value is not truly created with the end customer by making adjustments to a box or installing software. Don't drop a piece of technology on someone's desktop and expect to be awarded with a hug! The more likely user reaction will be, "Oh no, something new!," "what did you do to my ability to work!! I am lost – how does this work, what do I do now??!!" Complaints to management from workers etc. I have even seen unions get involved in this! People hate change. Your job is to create change. Unless you find a way to effectively include the people in the change, you will not be stellar! In fact, if you do not include the actual people who will be using the technology in it's implementation. you are more likely to have a disaster than a superb result.

This lesson seems particularly hard to get across to the smartest and most technical engineers. I have even seen a chaired computer science professor from a major Ivy League university totally not get this with a result of a system implementation being canceled.

Substantial resources were wasted and some careers took great damage because of his certitude that you could just order people into being competent with an arcane system. The majority of people just do not work that way.

22 – Personnel Unavailability

Projects that depend upon key personnel who have
a history of random unavailability.

There is little that is more destabilizing to a project than key personnel unavailable when you need them. Project schedules go up in smoke. Untold amounts of political capital may need to be spent to make up for Joe's frequent absence. It can make the whole project get confused! This problem can create broken promises to customers, impacts team morale, and is an overall nightmare. Obviously some of this is going to happen in real life. No one is always healthy. We all will occasionally run into things that create an unplanned absence. However, frequent absence is something else entirely.

The problem can be the random nature of the unavailability. The solution starts with a discussion with the personnel resource. Is the absence really random? Can it be made predictable? Sit down and talk with your staff members. You may learn of sickness, family problems or other personal problems. Try to make the random more predictable. Create a backup plan, including necessary personnel resources. Cross-training needed and ways to manage shared work. Given adequate resources, you as a project manager can plan for and accomplish just about anything. It is a good management plan to have cross-training as a matter of course. It is better to never let a single absence critically delay a project. Cross-training planned and implemented from the beginning of a project is the safest way forward. It is a good management plan to have cross-training as a matter of course. It is better to never let a single absence critically delay a project. Cross-training planned and implemented from the beginning of a project is the safest way forward. This is particularly true in the case of new or unusual technology. These skill sets may also be at a premium. You are actually reducing financial risk by planned cross-training.

23 – Rejected Contract Modifications

Projects where a customer refuses to modify the contract when the modifications appear to be logical, reasonable, and appropriate.

This is the kind of customer that you wish you could dispose of. There is something behind the scenes going on with this character. Some of the more probable causes include:

1. They are trying to get something for nothing (a thief).

2. A project manager who has created some problems on some other project that he/she is managing thus they are trying to now look super good to management.

3. They could not afford to do the project in the first place.

There maybe something else going on that is hidden from you and no one is talking to you about it. Customers will always try to get a bit extra, that is expected. A bit is one thing but a bit can be allowed for. A substantial revision in the scope of your work without funding to match is suicide for both you and your customer. It is possible that your customer is too new to project management to understand this. If you can, figure out a way to teach him or her, without making them look like a fool. Controlling scopes of work is discussed in further detail in other sections but for now, know that you must be strong regarding keeping the agreement or it is unlikely that you will be paid for your work.

Risk Factors Summary

If one were to take the above twenty-three risk factors the wrong way it will seem that there are hardly any safe projects of any size. And so it may be. But remember to use *judgment*. A substantial amount of money can be made on "risky" projects if they are handled right. A lot depends on successful assessment of risks and ameliorating the risks.

There are two basic paths to assessing and handling risk. These are:

1. To just know

2. To figure out

Strangely, both are valid. Just knowing means an intuitive knowledge or "gut feel" that something is a certain way, a feeling that you know is true, not just a hint. Nothing is wrong with that awareness but it is probably going to be a good idea to back it up with some solid evaluation.

The only real "weakness" with just knowing is that communication and confidence of others and self, in the "gut feel" may be too weak. Many people want identifiable, quantifiable reasons for everything. If convincing others or self is required, as is often the case, it is probably better to go ahead with "the building a case path". This path will provide enough evidence to justify your perceptions and thus gain support from others above and below you.

It is probably going to be necessary to "build a case" that states the exact factors that lead to an opinion about the level of risk of a particular project or path. This "case" then becomes the kernel of a justification to accept involvement in a project or to turn down a particular project or end one's involvement in it. Obviously, these are pretty important decisions so they should not be made without appropriate consideration.

One of the most effective methods I have ever found to evaluate project risk is to take the above 23 points and put them on a spreadsheet and rate the project in each category. Each category is given a weighted value of importance relative to the project and then a numeric risk level for that category is assigned. These are then multiplied to create a "weighted risk" for that category.

At the end of each spreadsheet the weighted risks for each of the 23 categories are averaged together. This creates an overall weighted average for this step of the project. At the end of the spreadsheet is a summary spreadsheet that averages together all of the weighted averages from each step of the project and ... "abra cadabra", an overall approximation of project riskiness is established. A sample spreadsheet is included at the end of this chapter for a project that involved updating the entire IT environment of a Federally chartered agency. This agency was mainly housed in a historic building and needed relatively secure connections for remote use. The point of these spread sheets is to provide a framework for risk analysis that does not miss anything major and provides a method to assess the risk of each project element. These risk judgments are then all added up and an overall grade is assigned in the summary spread sheet.

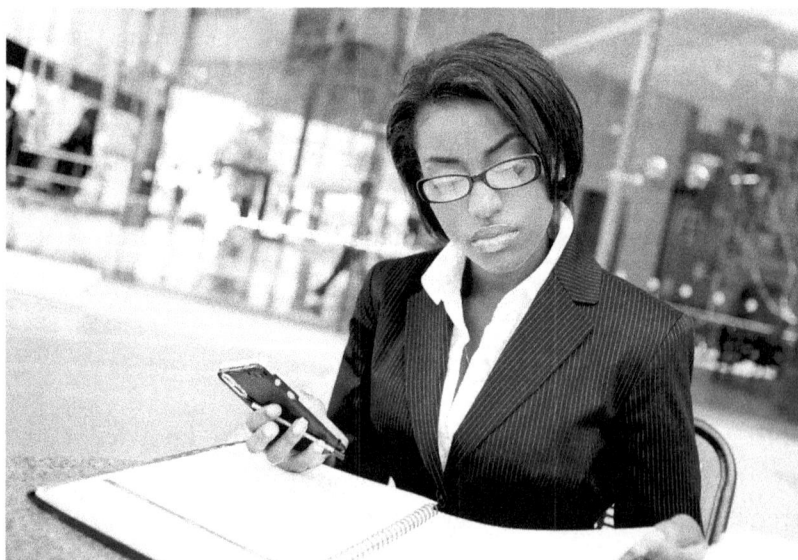

Is this a burdensome process? Well, yes somewhat. Does it help you to consider every aspect of what you are attempting in a structured way? – *yes* and that is critically important. Even more important, it provides you the opportunity to find risk mitigation strategies at a granular level and forecast their impact on the overall riskiness of the project. The two benefits mentioned above are substantial. Why? Because when you honestly assess risk at a granular level and apply the appropriate risk mitigation strategies you are not likely to be *surprised*! A decent manager, in a project with adequate resources and few surprises, can accomplish just about anything. Of course, liars can figure and figures can lie. As my statistics tutor once told me, "There are liars, damned liars, and then there are statisticians." The point is that numbers can blind people if you let them. This is something that any manager must be very cautious about in this day of computers and quantifiable data everywhere.

Do not, I repeat, do not take the lazy and apparently safe way out and let the numbers make the decision for you. The numbers are a guide and that's all – remember that. Contrary to what some people would have you believe, there are purposes beyond the mere creation of money. That is the purpose of a mint.

A company or organization succeeds when it is able to work on their stated mission without interference and hindrance. Yes, this takes money but it also takes intention to succeed and heartfelt drive most of all. This may not be obvious to you yet. But, ask any entrepreneur who has built a business and ask them if they did it just for the money. At some point, money is no longer an issue and all that keeps people going is desire and passion. When desire and passion are managed out of the business, ethics, real profit and business growth will diminish, possibly to nothing. In the end, project success all comes down to people keeping their word and doing what they have promised in a timely manner. This methodology is just one way to try to granulate all of the risk factors of a project and come up with a number that approximates likelihood of success.

Notes:

Sample Risk Factor Spreadsheets

The explanation below applies to the three risk tables.

First Column: Risk Factor

This is one of the risk factors discussed in the text of this chapter. Please see the appropriate chapter heading for a deeper review of a particular risk factor.

Second Column: Impact

Dangerousness to project success if this risk factor was to go very wrong. Sometimes in projects something can go very wrong and it has little impact on the project - this situation would be a 1 or a 2. While the impact of something else going wrong could have a high impact. For example, if new technology is critical to the success of a project then the impact of it not working would be very high. This probably warrants a 9 or 10 in the column.

Third Column: Relative Risk

This is a judgment call that you make after research of the likelihood of this risk factor coming into play. For example, you are likely to know if the project being considered is like something your company has done before. If you are running a shoe store and thinking of taking on a new manufacturer's line of shoes, you probably have a pretty good idea of what to look for and what type of marketing measures are required and how your customer base is likely to respond to the new styles etc. This familiarity may lead to a relatively low risk assessment, probably a 2 or a 3.

Fourth Column: Risk Value

This is simply the result of multiplying the second and third columns together. As stated in this chapter all of these risk values are eventually averaged together to provide a simple yet comprehensive estimate of overall perceived project risk.

As noted in the text, risk evaluation can be as granular as appropriate for a particular project. You can prepare one spreadsheet that encompasses the whole project or have multiple spreadsheets, potentially, one for each phase of the project. This example project has three major phases to demonstrate this concept.

Table 1 - Install Cable Network in a Building that is a National Historic Site			
Risk Factor	**A.** Impact Scale of 1 - 10	**B.** Relative Risk Scale 1 - 10	Risk Value A x B
1. Unlike anything your company has done before	8	10	80
2. Technology that has been on the market for less than 2 years	6	4	24
3. Includes technology that you don't have any experience managing	8	1	8
4. Large influx of new personnel within a short time line	0	0	0
5. Requires massive retraining of existing personnel	7	8	56
6. Relies upon technology from a financially weak vendor	0	0	0
7. Relies on a vendor with a poor record of customer service	0	0	0
8. Using a vendor whose executives have a poor track record of success	3	2	6
9. Relying on a vendor who has a poor record of technical success	0	0	0
10. Relying on technology from a vendor who will not make a priority service agreement	5	3	15

Risk Factor	**A.** Impact Scale of 1 - 10	**B.** Relative Risk Scale 1 - 10	Risk Value A x B
11. Relying upon technology from a vendor who will not let you communicate face to face with Sales Engineers, Sales Managers and Sales Reps	5	5	25
12. Your management is not enthusiastic about this project`	0	0	0
13. This project was oversold and the customer has ridiculous expectations	3	3	6
14. Projects with a weak customer project manager	6	4	24
15. When the customer does not care about timing	10	0.5	5
16. Projects that appear to be unbelievably profitable	10	0.5	5
17. A project that will be very hard to make profitable	10	0	0
18. Projects that are legally or contractually difficult	8	9	72
19. Crossing cultural boundaries especially from a long distance	8	9	72

Table 1 - Install Cable Network in a Building that is a National Historic Site

Table 1 - Install Cable Network in a Building that is a National Historic Site

Risk Factor	A. Impact Scale of 1 - 10	B. Relative Risk Scale 1 - 10	Risk Value A x B
20. Projects requiring participants with a variety of native languages	0	0	0
21. Projects that span many divisions of an organization	10	4	40
22. Personnel with a history of random unavailability	10	4	40
23. When the customer refuses to modify the contract when it is appropriate and logical to do so	10	0	0
Total Raw Score			**406**
Riskiness for this project step (406 divided by 23)			18

Table 2 - Capital Computer Workstation Install			
Risk Factor	**A.** Impact Scale of 1 - 10	**B.** Relative Risk Scale 1 - 10	Risk Value A x B
1. Unlike anything your company has done before	10	1	10
2. Technology that has been on the market for less than 2 years	10	3	30
3. Includes technology that you don't have any experience managing	10	2	20
4. Large influx of new personnel within a short time line	0	0	0
5. Requires massive retraining of existing personnel	3	8	24
6. Relies upon technology from a financially weak vendor	0	0	0
7. Relies on a vendor with a poor record of customer service	0	0	0
8. Using a vendor whose executives have a poor track record of success	3	2	6
9. Relying on a vendor who has a poor record of technical success	0	0	0
10. Relying on technology from a vendor who will not make a priority service agreement	5	3	15

Table 2 - Capital Computer Workstation Install			
Risk Factor	**A.** Impact Scale of 1 - 10	**B.** Relative Risk Scale 1 - 10	Risk Value A x B
11. Relying upon technology from a vendor who will not let you communicate face to face with Sales Engineers, Sales Managers and Sales Reps	5	0	0
12. Your management is not enthusiastic about this project`	0	0	0
13. This project was oversold and the customer has ridiculous expectations	8	6	48
14. Projects with a weak customer project manager	8	4	32
15. When the customer does not care about timing	10	0.5	5
16. Projects that appear to be unbelievably profitable	10	0.5	5
17. A project that will be very hard to make profitable	10	0	0
18. Projects that are legally or contractually difficult	8	0	0
19. Crossing cultural boundaries especially from a long distance	0	0	0

	Table 2 - Capital Computer Workstation Install		
Risk Factor	**A.** Impact Scale of 1 - 10	**B.** Relative Risk Scale 1 - 10	Risk Value A x B
20. Projects requiring participants with a variety of native languages	0	0	0
21. Projects that span many divisions of an organization	10	10	100
22. Personnel with a history of random unavailability	10	4	40
23. When the customer refuses to modify the contract when it is appropriate and logical to do so	10	0	0
Total Raw Score			**335**
Riskiness for this project step **(335 divided by 23)**			**15**

Worst possible raw score for any project element is 2200. This is pretty low risk - one would expect this to happen without too much pain.

Table 3 - Database Implementation			
Risk Factor	**A.** Impact Scale of 1 - 10	**B.** Relative Risk Scale 1 - 10	Risk Value A x B
1. Unlike anything your company has done before	10	5	50
2. Technology that has been on the market for less than 2 years	8	7	56
3. Includes technology that you don't have any experience managing	8	2	16
4. Large influx of new personnel within a short time line	0	0	0
5. Requires massive retraining of existing personnel	10	7	70
6. Relies upon technology from a financially weak vendor	10	0	0
7. Relies on a vendor with a poor record of customer service	10	1	10
8. Using a vendor whose executives have a poor track record of success	10	1	10
9. Relying on a vendor who has a poor record of technical success	10	3	30
10. Relying on technology from a vendor who will not make a priority service agreement	5	3	15

	A. Impact Scale of 1 - 10	B. Relative Risk Scale 1 - 10	Risk Value A x B
Table 3 - Database Implementation			
Risk Factor			
11. Relying upon technology from a vendor who will not let you communicate face to face with Sales Engineers, Sales Managers and Sales Reps	8	3	24
12. Your management is not enthusiastic about this project`	10	0	0
13. This project was oversold and the customer has ridiculous expectations	5	3	15
14. Projects with a weak customer project manager	6	4	24
15. When the customer does not care about timing	10	0.5	5
16. Projects that appear to be unbelievably profitable	10	0.5	5
17. A project that will be very hard to make profitable	10	4	40
18. Projects that are legally or contractually difficult	8	4	32
19. Crossing cultural boundaries especially from a long distance	0	0	0
20. Projects requiring participants with a variety of native languages	0	0	0

Table 3 - Database Implementation			
Risk Factor	**A.** Impact Scale of 1 - 10	**B.** Relative Risk Scale 1 - 10	Risk Value A x B
21. Projects that span many divisions of an organization	10	7	70
22. Personnel with a history of random unavailability	10	4	40
23. When the customer refuses to modify the contract when it is appropriate and logical to do so	10	3	30
Total Raw Score			542
Riskiness for this project step (406 divided by 23)			25

There is a definite level of risk in this step which requires strict management but still it is not so much to expect project failure.

Chapter 16 – Questions to Consider

1. How can you use this spreadsheet to evaluate project risk?

2. What is meant by risk amelioration?

3. Is it necessary to take some risk to make money or accomplish projects?

4. Think of examples of new technology that you have seen implemented. Have you observed any of the these risk factors and their impact?

5. What is the benefit to the risk factor list being granular?

6. Obviously, any one of the above factors could be its own chapter. Write up an example of some of them at work.

Chapter 17

The Tools of a Project Manager

∽ *For anyone seriously considering managing larger projects, it is strongly recommended that they become deeply familiar with software designed to assist project management.*

There is a short list of tools that a project manager needs to become capable of using. These include simple things like a PIM (personal information manager), or if you still like paper, a daily organizer. These tools help track meetings and agreements, as well as contacts. This category includes project management software that is often required by contract in larger projects. Recalling that the major tasks of a Project Manager are to communicate and to plan the execution of tasks, let us look at some tools that help a PM do both of these things. A critical part of the overall process of developing a project plan is breaking a large deliverable into smaller tasks. The small tasks are simply pieces of the overall project.

The relative worth of any of these tools can be measured by how well they help a project manager accomplish the dual-headed nature of the purpose of project management. Remember that all of these tools are just that, tools. A hammer is a tool too. How hard does one hit with a hammer? One hits as hard as one needs to. How many project management oriented tools does a project use? As many as they need to. Technology for the sake of itself is a wasted investment. This knowledge of how deeply to take a particular technique comes with education and experience. Education helps but real world experience is the best teacher in the use of these tools. Only by use will you master them.

We will briefly review the four of the major industry recognized tools in this section. They are:

1. The Gantt Chart

2. The Work Breakdown Structure

3. The Critical Path Model

4. The Program Evaluation and Review Technique

The Gantt Chart

The first is the famous Gantt chart. The Gantt chart is named after its creator, Henry L. Gantt . He formally documented this technique in 1910. This approach to organizing work has stood the test of time. It is probably the most used approach to organizing and communicating tasks to be performed, their relationships, and time factors involved in those tasks.

Some people call a Gantt chart a bar chart. Below is an example Gantt chart. In a Gantt chart tasks to be done are represented as a series of bars. The various bars show length of time scheduled for a given task. It is indeed useful but was created before things like desktop computers exist. Today more powerful tools exist, particularly for larger and more complex projects.

For anyone seriously considering managing larger projects, it is strongly recommended that they become familiar with software designed to assist project management. The most famous general purpose project management software package is probably Microsoft Project. There are other packages that are also quite effective.

The Work Breakdown Structure

The next tool is called the Work Breakdown Structure. This is known by the abbreviation WBS. The basic concept of WBS is to take an overall deliverable and break down the major accomplishments required to reach that deliverable into smaller accomplishments with a hierarchical numbering system that shows the relationships between the various smaller accomplishments and the major deliverable. For example, building a ship might include many sub deliverables. Perhaps the first is to build the hull of the vessel. In larger ships the hulls are sometimes created in sections. The overall hull assembly would receive the number 1.0, the first major subsection of the hull to be built would receive the number 1.1, the next major subsection would receive the number 1.2, the next 1.3, etc. until all of the major sections of the hull were numbered.

Next, the sub-deliverables that make up each part of each subsection would be numbered. For example, the first part of the first major subsection of the hull would be numbered 1.1.1, the second part of the first major subsection of the hull would be numbered 1.1.2, the third part of the first major subsection of the hull would be numbered 1.1.3 and so on. This process of breaking down into subsections can go indefinitely. This ability to be broken down indefinitely is both a strength and a weakness of this system. Project managers have to decide what level is appropriate for their use. One approach that can be useful is to combine the WBS system with the Gantt chart system. In essence, use WBS to break deliverables into smaller and smaller chunks and then when a particular chunk seems like it can be relatively easily broken down into a Gantt chart one simply does so and that is the end of the WBS breakdown for that deliverable.

There are few clear-cut answers. You are using a tool like a surgeon uses a scalpel, expertise comes with years of study and practice. This breaking down into smaller and smaller accomplishments can be detailed to the level required by the contract or the project manager, team or customer. This is simply a system of project analysis and documentation of work to be done. It is particularly useful on large and complex projects when they are managed with project management software. The value of the software tool becomes obvious as a delay in one task impacts other tasks and resources. The tool makes this slippage and its impact easier to see and think about. Thus, project software has a real value as a planning tool. Work Breakdown Structure is one of those curious tools that has value but can become so complex in actual use as to be more of a burden then a benefit. For very large projects, like building a ship, WBS can be very effective and is often required. For smaller efforts like managing the installation of a piece of software on twenty (20) computers, it is probably overkill to create a WBS document. The discipline of a WBS like activity is most useful in projects of large size.

The Critical Path Method

The following two pages demonstrate a Project Network Diagram which shows a great deal of information at one time. The most important thing about this type of diagram is that it shows the sequences of steps that can be done in parallel with each other while also showing the shortest possible path through the project with a particular set of task execution times. All of the steps on this shortest path is through the diagram are said to be on the critical path. This chart is called a Critical Path Method (CPM) diagram.

If any of these steps take longer than estimated, the whole project will be slowed down by the length of time the task exceeded its estimate. For example, if a critical path task was originally estimated to take 15 days and the task actually took 25 days then the whole project is likely to slow down by 10 days.

This diagram shows the critical path tasks to build our interstellar spacecraft that will take years to complete and the following milestones are on the critical path: Develop Thrusto Fuel, Develop Thrusto Warp Engines, Build Flux Transfer Hull and Assemble Engines to Hull.

If any of these "slip" (take longer than expected) the whole project will be slowed down. This could mean staff sitting around idle (burning up financial resources) waiting for the parts they need to show up etc. Thus, the project manager needs to be particularly aware of steps on the critical path to project completion.

Another valuable function a of CPM chart in project management software is it visually shows what happens when resources are added to a task that is on the critical path. In some cases it is possible to add enough resources to remove a task from the critical path completely. Sometimes doubling the staff will cut the calendar time required to accomplish a task in half. This could potentially remove a task from the critical path since cutting its time to complete in half may make another task more "critical" in this sense of time consumption.

It is very important that you as a project manager understand that adding personnel or other resources to a task does not mean it will be accomplished faster. In fact, the reverse can occur. Take a simple everyday task that we have experienced, say getting a haircut. Can you imagine the mess that could occur if half way through a haircut two more stylists were assigned to the same client? Maybe somewhere in Hollywood or something … not at my local hair place!

Generally the more creative and personal understanding the task requires the harder it is to "fix" a late task by adding resources; unless those resources can increase the productivity of the personnel already assigned to the task.

Sharp scissors help a stylist move faster, a more powerful computer help programmer speed up their programming, a cell phone that does not run out of battery will help a project manager communicate more effectively. When adding resources to try to speed a task be sure you communicate to those most familiar with the task about what is slowing them down. Frankly it's usually some kind of human or organizational problem but on occasion a new cell phone , or faster computer can make a world of difference!

Simple Critical Path Method

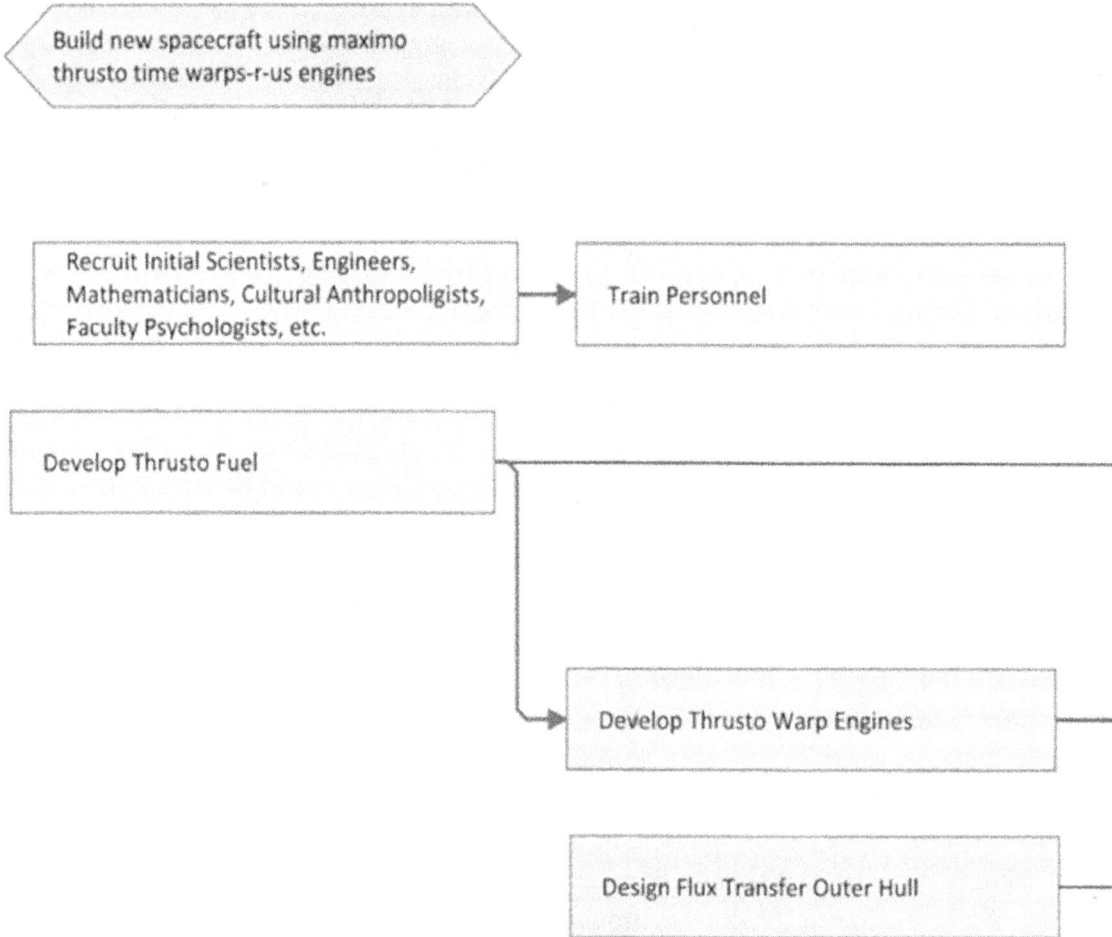

Build new spacecraft using maximo thrusto time warps-r-us engines

Recruit Initial Scientists, Engineers, Mathematicians, Cultural Anthropoligists, Faculty Psychologists, etc. → Train Personnel

Develop Thrusto Fuel

Develop Thrusto Warp Engines

Design Flux Transfer Outer Hull

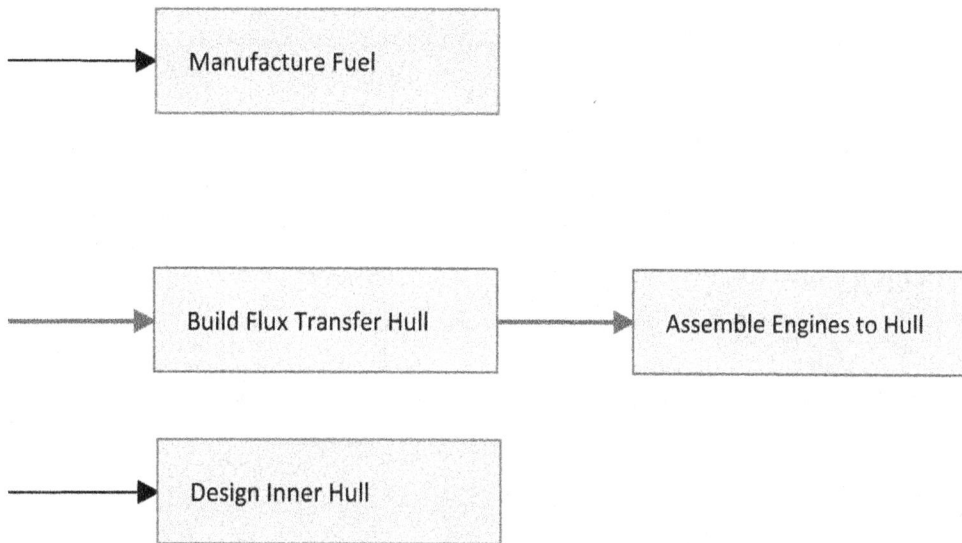

The Program Evaluation and Review Technique

Finally, there is the Program Evaluation and Review Technique method. PERT has many of the characteristics of the Critical Path Method.

The main difference is that in PERT, estimation of the time to complete a particular task is gathered from various sources. These are mathematically combined in an attempt to improve the accuracy of the overall network diagram. This approach more reliably detects the real world critical path. Pert improves the Critical Path Method by integrating multiple expert opinions. PERT is particularly worthwhile in dealing with areas where there is little more than educated conjecture regarding the length of time to complete a task. For example, if NASA were to try to develop a propulsion system for long-term space travel, various experts with the best available background might be called in to come up with time estimates. Then these estimates would be mathematically combined for each pertinent element of the project. Combining the best judgments that the best minds have to offer in a project plan.

The thing all of these charts have in common is that they are a way of graphically communicating relationships among tasks to complete. Once again, these tools have multiple purposes; planning and communication are the real purposes of all of these charts. Like most matters in project management, their value is relative to the task at hand.

Chapter 17 – Questions to Consider

1. *What is a Gantt Chart? What does it do well? Where might it start to lose effectiveness?*

2. *What is a Work Breakdown Structure? How deeply should you go with this type of tool? Can it be combined with other tools?*

3. *What is the Critical Path Model? Why is its use vital for projects with many interrelated elements?*

4. *What is Program Evaluation and Review Technique? What types of projects is PERT most appropriate for?*

Chapter 18

Change

 ❧ *Paradigm shifts are the real challenge for anyone involved in high tech. As a high tech professional, you must always watch out for new things that change everything.*

J ust as a species needs to be able to find a way to survive in its environment, either by changing it and conquering it or simply living off of the bounty it provides, so must a Project Manager be aware of and control the environment of a contract or project. In some ways, this is the hardest topic other than understanding the dual natured purpose of project management itself. There are two major types of change that you must deal with as a project manager. The first one, change in the project, is commonly discussed in project management texts while the second one seems to be overlooked. Perhaps it is just plain fear. The first, though challenging enough, is relatively easy to deal with once you understand it and have some experience with it. This is change in the project. This change is relatively easy to control. Because it is easy, we are going to discuss it second. Let's get the hard stuff out of the way first!

The Paradigm Shift

The harder change is termed a paradigm shift. Paradigm is a complex word for a simple concept. It means a particular method or approach to handling certain situations or the situations themselves. For example, most of us have a paradigm for how we get ourselves out to work or school in the morning. We know the environment in which we are working; (our living quarters) and we are familiar with its problems (are there any eggs in the refrigerator or are there any clean socks). We know lots and lots of information and what we don't know, we know how to find out (look in the refrigerator or the sock drawer). After some repeated attempts, we develop a process that will reach our goal of being out the door, in a reasonably presentable condition and at work on time. The process works, time and time again. It is reliable and helps us survive (get to work and get paid).

The impact of a paradigm shift is something to behold. Imagine that you got up one morning and still had sand in your eyes when you went to the bathroom to find it just wasn't there or it had so dramatically changed you were utterly confused. Suddenly you couldn't tell the sink from the bathtub or worse! That is a paradigm shift.

Imagine that you are one of the forms of life on the planet. You and those like you have been surviving for millions of years. You are participating in the normal activities of life; the cycle of life: birth, death, etc. and your type of life form survives over millions of years. Along comes a big rock from the sky and *blam*! The whole environment has shifted to one where your form of life does not now have tools to survive in the new environment. This is one probable cause of mass extinction. This is a paradigm shift of considerable size. How you used to survive just does not work anymore. Sheesh! The tough thing to understand for most people is that in high tech, paradigm shifts of magnitude occur on a regular basis. Skills that at times were very valuable, some years earlier have become nearly valueless.

Prior to 1981 there were numerous vendors of different types of computers. In fact, easily over 20 major computer manufacturers, many of whom had made major contributions to the industry in various ways. For example, take DataPoint Corporation. DataPoint was one of the first companies to make a commercially viable computer network. The price performance of their systems was remarkable. Have you ever even heard of them? Now we use the once special DataPoint coffee mug to dish out dog food. Ouch! How about Wang Corporation or DataGeneral or BasicFour? All of these companies are either gone or have shrunk so much as to be mere footnotes in history. Many people don't know it but even IBM had a substantial amount of trouble in the late 80's and early 1990s. So what was the paradigm shift that caused this? There were several enabling factors but the real paradigm shift was the dawn of the PC (personal computer) marketed by IBM. Suddenly, computer technology had become affordable, easier to purchase and applicable to everyday business life. So applicable, that if you did not have easy access to one of these things, you had substantial difficulty competing and surviving in an environment that was shifting to reflect the dominance of PC based technology. In less than five years, companies that were once dominant were closing their doors. The tens of thousands of technical personnel had to rapidly change their skills to the new environment or they could not compete and would lose the high incomes they and their families were used to. Entire stock portfolios became worthless. Retirement planning destroyed.

Paradigm shifts are the real challenge for anyone involved in high tech. As a high tech professional, you must always watch out for new things that "change everything." To make top dollar, you must keep your skill set tuned in the direction of the paradigm shift. The history of high tech appears to be a continuing series of paradigm shifts of varying magnitudes. The real challenge is staying aware of them, keeping your skills in alignment with them and creating tomorrow.

Those who have the skills that are needed during and after every paradigm shift bring top dollar until the shift is over. Then the value starts to drop off but is still substantial - at least until the next paradigm shift.

The project management skills evolved and documented in this book have been through at least four paradigm shifts and have been proven applicable in all of them. Thus, they probably have long term value. Much like having a blood stream appears to be of long time value to a large species surviving on dry land - at least in the environment as we know it!

The lessons here are:

- What paradigm shifts are and that they are real and often happen in high tech.

- That they can be very dangerous to your career or your project.

- That you can use them to advance your career and your project.

- That you must constantly be aware of what is happening in the technology marketplace.

- That you must keep your skills attuned to what is needed in the marketplace.

In essence, try not to get caught unaware. Read the trade journals appropriate to your field. Go to as many manufacturer sponsored seminars as possible. Join the appropriate professional associations, go the meetings, become involved. These are the kinds of activities that will keep you aware of what is coming.

A concrete example may help to further illustrate the point. Many years ago the author of this book was a systems analyst and computer programmer for a major consulting company. Years earlier in my career, I had attended training on and was somewhat familiar with DataPoint Corporation's networking products but did not consider myself an expert. I had some slight familiarity.

A vice-president of the consulting firm where I was employed called a meeting and asked all of the technical personnel to raise their hands if they had background in computer networking – no one raised their hands. His comments were expletives. Then he said, "Doesn't someone have at least a little bit of background?" I realized this was an opportunity so I raised my hand saying I had just a bit. He said, "Good! You are now our expert!" I was shocked and then later, laughed hysterically. This was ridiculous Me, an expert on a topic I had only slight familiarity with? But, it resulted in a major opportunity to become familiar with this type of technology. I eventually became certified in this area and it fed my family quite well. Of course, today, networking computers is generally easy.

Here are two paradigm shifts. The first was the coming of small computer networking where the skills became extremely valuable and the second was the undoing of the first where the process of computer networking itself was made so easy that all of the extremely technical skills were no longer in great demand by the market.

Near the beginning of the networking boom, I could literally make a phone call and get a new job with a twenty percent raise. I did this twice in 3 years. If my boss was rude or unreasonable, I walked and got more money – sweet! My salary went up by forty percent over three years! Then the other shift happened. Networking became easier to accomplish and the same overall skill set is worth far less. It is still an important skill set but the skill set is now more commonplace. Paradigm shifts mean a lot to you and to your projects. The reason I was able to get that high salary was because people needed my skill set to make their projects work. There were few resources available that could do the work so the value of the skill set naturally increased. Then there were other paradigm shifts and the value of the skill set dramatically dropped.

The other topic of this section is managing change in the microcosm we call a project. Just as a species needs to be able to find a way to survive in its environment, either by changing it and conquering it or simply living off of the bounty it provides, so must a Project Manager be aware of and control the environment of a contract or project. Earlier we discussed the resources that a PM must control to accomplish the goal of project management. It is also true that these resources make up the main elements of the environment of a project. Largely, what a project manager is doing is manipulating the various factors in the project environment so that people can produce and get things done and create future projects (marketing and sales - critically important). Because the environment is composed of these particular resources, we now have a way of evaluating the impact of paradigm shifts on a project. Simply consider the impact on these resources and you can create a reasonable prediction of the future.

For example, say a technical resource upon whom you rely has been given an offer that you just cannot match. There is no way that the project budget can compete with the new higher salary offer. This key resource is going to go and unfortunately, there is little you can do about that. So what is the impact of the loss of Joe and how do you as a PM handle it? Pull out the chart of twenty resources and evaluate the impact against each of the resources. What other resources will be impacted by the loss of this personnel? What resources can you use to minimize the impact? What should you do to go forward and replace the resource or perhaps not replace the resource or perhaps cancel the project?

To handle these types of problems look at them from a perspective of resource utilization and it will help reduce the stress and put you in a position where you can more calmly figure out what is the best way forward relative to accomplishing the dual purposes of project management.

Then everyone wins. Worry about how irreplaceable a particular resource is and you will be playing the fool. If you become overwhelmed over the loss of a particular resource, your management, your customers, your other employees and even yourself will eventually come to feel you are no longer effective as a project manager. Your job and self-confidence are history.

Pick a more workable approach such as the one explained above and you have a method of how to go forward. No method, no problem solving approach, no path to help bring order to the chaos - your life just got much tougher. Apparently, the dinosaurs went extinct because they could not handle such dramatic change in their resource environment. Please note well, that this change is not always easy. Depending upon the size of the environmental shift, it can be truly challenging to overcome. But at least you have a path to follow, a way forward that is known to work if it is employed.

According to some paleontologists, birds are probably some of the last remaining remnants of the great dinosaurs. Perhaps those dinosaurs that were most bird like survived because they were able to use their resources (their ability to fly) to change to different environments, as needed and some managed to survive. It must have been terrible. Yet apparently, eggs were still laid, enough managed to hatch and be fed to bring on the next generation until the environment became friendly enough for mass proliferation of the new species that we now call birds.

As a high technology project manager, you must constantly be aware of the importance of successful change and do whatever it takes to create that. In the case of man surviving in the wild, his environment is whatever he can see with his eyes, smell with his nose, taste, touch, and perhaps feel in other sensory channels. That is the environment that a man or woman must survive in and that is their "problem space." It is where they solve the problems of survival. Modern business life does not appear anything like life in the jungle or the primeval forest. Yet the things that make up the daily life of a project manager are just as dangerous as animals in the jungle, just not as obviously so. When one is bitten by a rattle snake, one is in for some trouble. In the wild environment, one listens for the rattle and avoids it or attacks it. One observes the environment and adjusts things based upon observation, either changing the environment or adapting to it as appropriate.

Today, most of us live in sprawling urban environments. We have jobs and we earn money with which we buy things like food. Our survival is less predicated upon the keenness of our observation of the immediate environment. Or is it? Perhaps all that has really happened is that, due to a series of paradigm shifts, our environment has just shifted to a point that we don't realize we are still surviving in an environment. We live in houses or apartments of steel and stone, we buy our food at grocery stores and restaurants. But if we do not have skills and the ability to exchange them for food and housing, we cannot survive any more than a Velociraptor did after the planet was hit by a massive meteor. A paradigm shift is a paradigm shift no matter the cause. Today, a brilliant project manager is very aware of the environment just as a brilliant hunter is! The difference is different things make up the environment.

What are the key things that make up a project manager's environment and are they important? For a project manager, the single most critical element of the environment is the set of rules that defines success and failure. That set of rules is called a contract. The contract is the biggest part of the environment that a project manager must understand. Sometimes that contract has been read by expensive lawyers and sometimes it is "just an assignment" from one's own company. It makes no real difference. The contract still makes the rules. Every contract and project, to some degree, sets its own paradigm. It contains a description of the game to be played to reach survival (getting paid). If the team does not accomplish the contract then there is no pay and thus no food on the table, no money to pay the electric bill, etc. Not all that different from the jungle after all, is it?

Contract Changes

Just as the environment can change, so can a contract change. If you keep track of those changes and use them to your advantage, you will be somewhat successful as a project manager. This is comparable to a herd of buffalo migrating to new pastures when the old has been consumed. As long as there is plenty of pasture, the herd will flourish,. As long as there are plenty of projects, this style of project management will succeed too. If you cause those changes and see to it that they occur in a way that promotes the accomplishment of the dual nature of project management, you will be very successful as a project manager. This is comparable to a farmer planting and caring for his animals and thus earning a more stable life. Higher still would be the farmer advanced enough to use irrigation and fertilizer and that is where we are trying to go!

If you completely ignore change in a contract you are likely to fail. How is a project or a contract successfully changed? And just as important, how is all of this change controlled? Normally, in a contract between two parties, the contract change procedure is defined in the original contract. In an internal project there is (or should be) a formal change control process that has been implemented by management. The two project types (internal and external) are similar but the external change control process usually has a few more steps. The contract change process may include steps that require document inspection/endorsement by a lawyer and senior management endorsement. This is less likely to occur with internal projects.

What are some of the key factors that should be present in virtually all change control systems? Here is a list:

- Why is it necessary?

- Why should we spend the money?"

- Priority and impact – How important is it and what will happen if it is not done? – a different way of saying "why should we spend the money."

- Time Factors – "Does it need to be finished urgently?" – a different way of saying why should we spend the money on overtime or hire additional resources to get it done quickly.

Evaluation of impact on:

- Overall schedule and due dates

- On other tasks

On resources required including:

- Personnel

- Finances

- Hardware

- Software

- The data communications environment

- Other infrastructure impacts such as backup and restore of data and disaster recovery.

Authorizations required such as:

- Levels of funding

- Below a certain funding level, one tier of management can authorize

- Above that, two tiers of management are required to authorize

- Possibly, so on, up to the President/Chief Executive Officer of a firm

- Signatures of both customer PM and contractor or performer PM or more senior management.

Multiple signatures maybe involved when the end user must authorize, the budget people must authorize, and the management of the performer of the work must authorize. Sometimes multiple departments are involved and signatures must be obtained from all departments involved. This can get quite time consuming! So allow plenty of time for authorization processes in complex situations.

Other systems may be impacted by the modification. This can involve a systems analyst's review of the systems involved to minimize chance of unexpected impact. For example:

- Down time may need to be scheduled in advance

- Users may require retraining because of changes in various systems that interface with the system being changed

Finally, some change management system must actually hold the original documents and there should probably be on-line access to such documents. There is a great deal to consider when working with change management. One must always have some sort of system of change management. It does not always have to be complex but it does need to be effective at helping to control change and seeing to it that all changes are approved as appropriate and that the impact of all changes is thoroughly considered before the changes are started.

Below is a sample change request form based on one used in the world of information systems.

Sample Change Request

Name of Project = Change Request CR # _____

Prepared by: _____ Date Submitted:

Title: _____

Enter a brief, descriptive name for this change request.

Priority

Use a one or two word description of the change request priority (e.g., Top, High, Medium or Low).

Change Request Details

Describe the change being requested. Include a description of impacts to existing objectives and deliverables as well as any new objectives and deliverables.
A change request should include a justification which should include:
1. Provide a business case for the change request
2. Impact if not implemented
3. Discuss any issues of timing of implementation.

Change Request Impact Analysis

Scope & Requirements

Describe the impacts on project requirements including whether this is in or out of the scope of the project..

Project Risk

Describe risks associated with this change or overall impacts of change on project risks.

Schedule

Describe potential impacts of change on project schedule. Include description of proposed implementation schedule associated with this change.

Budget

Include information about impacts on project budget. Provide specific details on costs associated with the change.

Project Management

Describe any impacts to the project management plan or project organization

Resolution Description

Include information about what is to happen with this change request (e.g., approved, denied, on hold, etc.), the date this decision was made, who was involved in the decision and the rationale for the decision.

Alternatives

Describe alternatives to the proposed change.

Request Implementation Activities

Describe specific follow-on activities required by the resolution, assigned resource, time line and other details. Include references to modifications to the project schedule and project or project management deliverables as appropriate. Describe specific follow-on activities required by the resolution, assigned resource, time line and other details. Include references to modifications to the project schedule and project or project management deliverables as appropriate.

Recommendation

Include a recommendation of proposed action based on recommended change and impacts.

Chapter Eighteen – Questions to Consider

1. *What is meant by the term paradigm shift?*

2. *Why is change management an opportunity?*

3. *What information must be tracked for effective change management?*

4. *How does a good project manager use project change to the advantage of both the client and project personnel?*

5. *Name two results of projects not having change management in place.*

Chapter 19

The Adoption of Technology

> ∽ *Ridiculous amounts of money have been spent replacing systems that actually worked just fine but were not adopted by users due to inadequate orientation to the system and inadequate training. In the end, a fight for training time and user orientation time is a fight for value.*

How does one create the adoption of technology? In some ways, this question is the most important question discussed in this book. Until technology is effectively adopted, it has no value. No value equals no exchange and that means that the people who are implementing the technology have effectively become thieves. Perhaps, a little harsh but completely true. This is one of the reasons that executives are hesitant to invest in new technology – lack of value created.

Creating the effective adoption of technology is just about the same thing as creating value. So what goes into this? How does one create the effective adoption of technology, and how does this work with the dual headed nature of the purpose of project management?

The Key Elements

These factors are discussed below.

1. Have a product that can actually provide useful value to people

2. Let people know that it has this real useful value

3. Help people adopt the technology

4. Continue to refine the useful product so it provides more value

5. Continue to see that it is adopted and used

There is an amazing amount of work that goes into the creation of having a truly useful product. In high tech, that normally includes a series of steps and actions ranging from market needs analysis to systems design and rapid prototyping, software implementation through various marketing activities, and finally, sales and customer support. Microsoft is an example of a company that knows how to do this well. It can be argued that they overdo it but they certainly do it!

The point is that whatever product you have, whether it be software or paper plates, it must be a real product that someone can and will use to enhance their life or accomplish their purposes in some way. Otherwise, there is no exchangeable value. It can be a video game, an airplane, or a tube of lipstick - anything someone considers serves a useful purpose. The next major point is to let people know that it exists and can provide them value. You must get into communication with various publics and demonstrate the product to them. This is an active, almost evangelical, process. If this all sounds like a marketing campaign then you have the right idea.

People use things because they believe that those things will aide their survival in some way. Your job is to let them know that your project team has something that will do just that and demonstrate its value to them. Even if the implementation of your product has been ordered from the highest levels of an organization, unless people believe the product will help them, the uptake of the product will be slow or non-existent and there will be little or no value delivered to the consuming organization.

Earlier I mentioned an accounting system I was working on for an organization that will remain nameless. The person in charge of the IT (Information Technology) for this global organization held a doctorate from Harvard (or was it Princeton or Yale?) in Computer Science, no less. He was an absolute genius of technology but had trouble with the idea that systems had to be marketed to end users and that orders from headquarters would not be enough to see the system put into use.

I tried to explain the facts of technology uptake in organizations to this PhD. He refused to understand. It took them many years and several rewrites of the software to get this software implemented properly and in use. This was a very strong organization with effective command and control structures in place, but even they failed to force into use systems that technically worked but were relatively unresponsive to user needs and were not marketed well internally!

A good product, marketed well will always win. A technically good product that is difficult to use or does not truly address the problems of the end user community and is not well marketed is a nearly certain failure. So it was and probably always will be as long as people have the free will to act!

The Communication of Value

This means explaining the potential value of something and demonstrating it to staff and executives. Sometimes it means holding a meeting or publishing an announcement or article in a company journal. Communication!

The process is:

1. Finding the value for each and every public that might use a system and communicating to them about it

2. Seeing to it that they recognize the potential value

3. Bringing that potential value into reality by helping people adopt the technology

4. Continuing to refine the product so it provides more value

5. Continue to see that it is adopted and used

There are probably ten thousand ways that a person could get a team to communicate about a project, a good project manager is creative and capable in many spheres of activity. He or she does not have to be a genius at anything but must be able to create value by using many different facilities and capabilities. Perhaps this is their genius: drive, desire, the ability to communicate, and the creativity and insight into using many different channels of communication to accomplish the dual-headed purpose of project management.

Help People Adopt the Technology

A project plan that includes funding and tasks to help people adopt technology is something that will create value more than almost any other factor in all of high tech. That is quite a claim and it is a true one. If the product of a project is not in use then the project is not providing major value. Thus, getting technology into use is more important than the technology itself. Unfortunately, most customers do not understand this. They seem to focus on features rather than benefits. This is an extremely large mistake that many people make. Put your attention on value creation. Create as much value as you can with the budget you have and you have won! This does not say develop as many features as you can and use every single penny you have on programmers and computer resources. What it means is spend what you must on programmers and computers and technical development *but* leave money for user orientation and user training! Value comes from utilization. If people are not trained to utilize your product or do not understand why they ought to, then the potential for value creation is minimized!

Ridiculous amounts of money have been spent replacing systems that actually worked just fine but were not adopted by users due to inadequate orientation to the system and inadequate training. I have actually observed this, several times in different organizations. There appears to be a form of insanity in groups that says to not spend money on training and orientation to systems. Training for staff is one of those items that are easily cut in budget meetings. It is much "easier" to cut training than raise the cost of employee health care by 10 dollars per month. The result of this illogical thinking is often a situation something like this: We can afford twenty new computers at a cost of forty thousand dollars but we cannot allow more than fifteen minutes of orientation to the new accounting system running on those computers. This, of course, means that the accounting clerks will have to figure it out for themselves, making many mistakes in the process and generally building up frustrations while injuring the reputation of the overall project that built it and certainly minimizing the value created. In the end, a fight for training time and user orientation time is a fight for value.

Continue to Refine the Useful Product so it Provides More Value

Congratulations! The widgets are completed and people have been oriented and trained to use them, they are being used and value is being created big time. You are a success; but could things be better? Yes, in fact, they could! It is a super idea to have some time in a project to refine a product so it more closely approaches the ideals of the consuming publics. Now we are getting up to a superlative level of value creation. Make something good, get it in use, then make it better, and get it in broader use. The greater the utilization the greater the value you are creating! Of course, that means that you must once again continue the orientation and training process with the latest features so they can be used and their values are recognized.

Summary

This too is a kind of rising expanding spiral. The more that users are trained and capable with a system, the more they will use it and become more productive because of it. This then creates demand for the system to be even more effective. When this is accomplished, users must be trained again and it just goes on and on potentially for years. Thus, follow on contracts are created because the orientation and training gave the users the confidence and competence to use the systems in the first place!

Chapter Nineteen - Questions to Consider

1. *What is value really?*

2. *How is it created?*

3. *Is ordering a new product into use the best way to get it used?*

4. *What is the most important part of creating value in high tech projects?*

Chapter 20

Closing the Project

> ∾ *The turnover is one of the final deliverables of value and should be well handled. It is, after all, a chance for your staff to show off their creations.*

Managing the project is largely balancing resources with the needs of the Statement of Work while seeing to it that one is accomplishing the dual natured purpose of project management. Great job. You and your team did it. Now we are at the final step of closing the project.

Closing the Project

Are you ready for a surprise? In some ways this is the most difficult part of the project. There are several things that must be accomplished in this phase. Some of these are human resources related, some are legal, some are heart wrenching, some are heartwarming. The main things that have to be dealt with in project closure are resource issues, user training if not dealt with earlier, final accounting and getting the legal acceptance.

Handling Resource Issues

The first thing you must know is that in the last two months of major projects that are done by contract, practically all of the staff involved on the contract will be looking for their next job. This may be in the existing company or with a different company. This may include you, the PM. One can be quite torn in these situations. You have a fiduciary responsibility to see the project through and a responsibility to see to it that you and your family has a roof over its head. Depending upon a variety of factors, many of which you may have little or no control over, your job may be about to end. That is the real world and that is hard to handle. Most companies do not keep personnel as expensive as project managers sitting around for very long at all. Do not be surprised if you are given your walking papers within two weeks of the end of the project. This is particularly true if your organization is a contract-oriented company. Thus, you may be listening to your whole staff nearly ready to revolt while you are trying to get the last of the work finished. It is a hard time emotionally and can be physically draining. It is never easy. But, if you have followed the dual nature of PM, you and your staff's reputation should be in excellent condition. Your customer or your company may even help your personnel find new jobs.

The point is your project plan needs to allow a great deal of slack time during the end because your formerly loyal and effective personnel may well be out looking for their next job. You may be too! All of the real hard work should have been done long before the end of the project/contract. Plan it any other way and you are asking for an absolutely horrible situation. The last thing you want to be involved in is the debacle of most personnel disappearing with much of the work left to be done. Trying to hire high quality personnel and get them oriented and productive into an position with less than three months of work available is normally quite difficult. This is a horrible situation and can consume and waste any and all political capital you may have created.

The moral is: get it done early! Then it is easy to give your folks part of a day to go to an interview. Even better, it can all be done openly and honestly. Perhaps you can even use your own staff for a recommendation. The worst case scenario is to pretend the situation does not exist when you know it does. Truly, all anyone ever got from sticking their head in the sand was sand in their eyes. Prepare for this situation in advance and get things done long before the end of the contract and most everyone on the project will win including the customer! End load the project plan and you, your reputation, your company, your staff, and probably your family will suffer.

Final Testing, Turn Over, and Acceptance

Final testing must be a well-planned activity, with all tests thoroughly thought through and documented as acceptance criteria in the Statement of Work. Final testing must be completed in advance of the turn over date and most of all there should be *no surprises*. If something is not going to pass tests then all should know about it before the tests. In that case an agreement should be made in advance of the final test date. Usually agreements and negotiations can handle the occasional item that just will not work as originally envisioned. A fictitious example is the space ship will only reach 1.5 times the speed of light (instead of the hoped for 1.7) when nothing before ever even came close to the speed of light. People can deal with such matters when they are known about in advance.

Next, we have the final training and turn over to the customer. What is hard here is to see to it that your staff still has a caring attitude even though they know they may be unemployed in two or three weeks. This can be tough for all concerned. Yet, it can also be the setting of the final jewel of value in the project. As has been mentioned so many times, unless the product is utilized, it is not providing value. The turnover is one of the final deliverables of value and should be well handled. It is, after all, a chance for your staff to show off their creations. This turn over needs to be a well organized affair. There may even be a dinner afterwards!

Now back to closing the project itself. This is the time of the Final Accounting! Where did all of the resources go? Do you have it fully documented? Are the lawyers happy? Did you make a profit in the end? Does the customer have all of the documentation the contract agreed to give them? Etc. You need to start dotting all of the I's and crossing all of the T's long before the closure of the contract because you will need all of those details to hand at contract closure. Getting customer final acceptance often has to do as much with the paperwork of a project as it does with the widget that was created for the customer. Are all building inspection reports completed, product warranties completed etc. This is where all of that blasted tracking and attention to detail pays off. When you finally show up with the package of documentation all neatly organized with a ribbon around it, in a beautifully presented binder, the customer knows they have been given a professional job. Compare that scenario to showing up for the "final" meeting with papers a mess and serial numbers half missing – what a mess. This is the kind of thing that creates jobs for lawyers - but not a future for a project manager. Part of the work of a superlative PM is to avoid the excessive need for lawyers in the first place.

Chapter Twenty – Questions to Consider

1. *Why is this the most difficult time of the project?*

2. *What kind of loyalty should you expect from your staff at this time and why?*

3. *What should you be doing at this time?*

4. *When does project paperwork need to be updated and easily made ready for delivery?*

5. *When should test plans be established?*

6. *Why is this important?*

7. *Should you help your personnel find their next position?*

Chapter 21

Final Thoughts

> ∾ *A good project manager is extremely responsible, extremely creative, cares about others and their work and demands performance from self and others and gets the job done!*

One must recognize that projects are organic wholes, almost with a life of their own. You as the PM are somewhat the brain of the project or the being in charge if you wish. It is up to you to keep the whole thing moving forward while creating the future and a win-win game for all concerned. It is a challenge and is not easy to do. That is why you are paid the big bucks. You must see to it that the change orders are kept up, that deviations from the project plan are understood and corrected or the plan amended and funding found for the deviations. You must run the shop! You must make a profit and deliver the goods and indeed maintain the image of the whole project. This is a daily balancing act. It depends more upon your ability to effectively communicate to all of the key players than any other ability. You can keep the numbers perfectly straight but if you don't effectively communicate the numbers to your customer's PM then they don't exist. You must keep your personnel motivated to a high degree of professionalism while allowing for the foibles of the human condition. You must help dream the big dream and inspire everyone to dream it with you, without looking too corny while you do it! You must be just and fair and make a profit! This is all done by balancing the resources noted above according to the dual nature of project management.

Remember the Dream

I hope you have found this text enjoyable and informative. I suggest you keep it on hand and reread it whenever you feel it might help.

Remember the dream!

A Project manager is a creator of the highest order of magnitude. It is not well recognized in our society because we expect artists to wear berets and have outlandish clothes and sometimes outlandish behavior patterns. But always remember you are a person who has the guts and the responsibility to change the reality of everyday life for people. That makes you something special – you have the guts to do something about it!

This is not meant to decry the value of music nor a painting. Rather it is meant to raise the stature of a good PM to where it belongs. A good PM is extremely responsible, extremely creative, cares about others and their work, demands performance from self and others, and gets the job done! All the while, the best PMs are following the dual-natured purpose of project management and creating a new future.

Always remember:

The Purpose of Project Management

      ∽   *The purpose of project management is to manage the creation of the perceptions related to a project as well as managing the creation of the deliverables of a project*

Thank you for reading this book and may your life be enhanced from it!

Notes:

List of Image Credits

Frontispiece
ID 78010874 © Ratz Attila on Dreamstime.com
(modified by the book designer)

Pg. 7 – Twins
ID 4209005 © Chode on Dreamstime.com

Pg. 12 – Business Gradient Color Graph Bar
ID 37963932 © Heromen30 on Dreamstime.com

Pg. 23 – Building a New Creative Idea
ID 37240991 © Alphaspirit on Dreamstime.com

Pg. 30 – People with Direction
ID 41933283 © Digitalstormcinema on Dreamstime.com

Pg. 34 – Silhouettes of Business People Working and Speech Bubbles...
ID 41013509 © Rawpixelimages on Dreamstime.com

Pg. 39 – A Chicken Lays an Egg and There is Money Inside
ID 70885780 © Koragit Chaipanha on Dreamstime.com

Pg. 40 – Time is Money
ID 59546144 © Pogonici on Dreamstime.com

Pg. 43 – Time Management
ID 36236786 © Kosecki11 on Dreamstime.com

Pg. 58 – Fast Time
ID 34340428 © Alain Lacroix on Dreamstime.com

Pg. 65 – Help in your Business
ID 32287175 © Alphaspirit on Dreamstime.com

Pg. 70 – Multi-Ethnic Business People Working in Team
ID 44049532 © Rawpixelimages on Dreamstime.com

Pg. 76 – Teamwork Business Team Meeting Unity Jigsaw Puzzle Concept
ID 47350521 © Rawpixelimages on Dreamstime.com

Pg. 80 – Key Management Business Asset
ID 17331370 © Dave Bredeson on Dreamstime.com

Pg. 86 – Teamwork
ID 29771604 © Alphaspirit on Dreamstime.com

Pg. 95 – Risk in Business
ID 43952036 © Sergey Khakimullin on Dreamstime.com

Pg. 117 – Boundaries and Complexities
Author and Book Designer

Pg. 120 – Black Business Woman Photo
ID 4602958 Stephen Coburn on Dreamstime.com

Pg. 135 – Project Management with Gantt Chart
ID 38721581 © Leung Cho Pan on Dreamstime.com

Pg. 138-139 – CPM Chart
Author and Book Designer

Pg. 142 – Urban Construction
ID 43856219 © Sergey Khakimullin on Dreamstime.com

Pg. 152 – Technology Migration
ID 41736734 © Alphaspirit on Dreamstime.com

Pg. 160 – Balance Concept
ID 43983990 © Sergey Khakimullin on Dreamstime.com

About the Author

I decided to write this book because I was frustrated with inappropriate management decisions. I have seen millions of wasted dollars and far too many frustrated users and upset technical personnel. Too often technology is implemented in a way that does not create as much value or help people as much as it could. I simply despise seeing wasted and ineffective effort because of project management deficiencies. Project management is often not easy, but with the methodologies I have developed and laid out in this book, it is easier to accomplish your goals and deliver real value to all concerned. That is what this book is about, creating real value and success!

By today's standards I started in the activities of business and showed an entrepreneurial spirit at a very young age. I was selling vegetables from the family garden door to door when I was 6 years old. I was part of the family shoe businesses by the age of 16. These were classic small businesses: I cleaned floors and toilets, built inventory shelves and seasonal displays, did stockroom work, created catalogs and in our business, sold shoes.

Eventually, I attended and graduated from The George Washington University with a Bachelor's degree in Business specializing in Information Systems Technologies. While at GWU, I computerized my family's retail shoe stores to further enhance our excellent customer service and make us more competitive. I was making decisions that involved, for a small family business, truly substantial amounts of money. These decisions required an even stronger technical understanding. Therefore, I talked my way into classes in the College of Computer Science; including programming in binary and microcircuit design. This substantial technical background has helped me throughout my career.

When my father decided to sell the family business to Johnston and Murphy Shoe Company, my career in creating, managing and implementing computer systems took off. My professional experience grew to include managing projects in both software development and computer networking. Later I became president of my own company which provided software and services to the U.S. Department of Education and the Department of Defense and the Federal Aviation Administration. Factually, my awards and commendations could fill a wall.

This success led to managing international commercial projects and I later began teaching project management in Asia as they had a desire to understand modern western project management. I taught in China, South Korea, and other Asian countries; course delivery expanded to include Australia, Europe, South America and the US. There was never enough time in class, so students and I would go out for dinner late into the night to discuss the issues of technology and project management. Experience managing projects and teaching project management across many cultures helped me prove the ideas and the project management approach put forth in this book.

My professional technical certifications include Microsoft Certified Professional ID # 316 and two different Microsoft Certified Systems Engineer certifications, plus a variety of other professional certifications.

About the Author

This book, like my life, is no armchair discussion of project management theory. It and I are about actually getting the job done with value created for all concerned, happy customers and staff looking forward to our next project. I hope you find this book an interesting and fresh look at business and project management. These techniques and approaches will help you fulfill your desires for professional success, enhance your career and help your customers and staff. Enjoy the voyage!

A. Mark Massey
July, 2017
MarkMassey.org

Colophon

The interior book design done in Adobe InDesign®.

   The typefaces used are Adobe Caslon Pro, Minion Pro and Microsoft San Serif. Adobe Caslon Pro is a revival of Caslon, based on William Caslon's original specimen pages printed between 1734 and 1770. Minion was designed by Robert Slimbach in 1990 for Adobe Systems and was inspired by late Renaissance-era type. Microsoft Sans Serif is a True Type font used in the tables in Chapter 16, — The Twenty Three Risk Factors.

Cover Design

The cover design utilized Adobe Photoshop® and Adobe InDesign®.

   The eagle and chess figures were painted in Photoshop® and then added to a personal photograph. Then the entire image was transferred to InDesign® for the final product.

   You can contact Darlene Massey at her website: DreamSpaceDesign.com

Notes: